Fire Song is a wonderful read due in which it is written. The book i in a very engaging dialogical manner, and on page after page the reader is treated to a nourishing banquet of ideas that really matter—ideas about truth, meaning, value, God, the soul, and life after death. I highly recommend it.

– **JP Moreland**, Distinguished Professor of Philosophy, Biola University and author of The Kingdom Triangle

"It's the most important message we have from God... It's called the Gospel. Yet, even most Christians really don't understand it or appreciate it. It's so much bigger than our salvation! Thanks, John, for helping others see that too!"

– **Frank Pastore**, host of "The Intersection of Faith and Reason," on KKLA in Los Angeles.

Fire Song is engaging from the very first page. It speaks directly to our generation by weaving an ancient narrative into our postmodern world. John Mitchell asks all the right questions to help reignite in us the ancient song that brings us home. Read it. This book may just change your life!

– **Dave Stone**, Intrigue Films

John Mitchell gives us an inspirational and thoughtful account of belief based on reason. Fire Song is an intelligent and thought provoking approach to a subject so central to our existence.

– **Daryn** and **Megan Colledge**

FIRE SONG

REDISCOVERING THE ANCIENT MELODY

John A. Mitchell

FORWARD BY

Johnny Meier

ENDURANCE PRESS

2012

Fire Song is available at special quantity discounts
for bulk purchase for sales promotions, premiums,
fund-raising, and educational needs. For details write
Endurance Press, 577 N Cardigan Ave Star, ID 83669.

Visit Endurance Press' website at www.endurancepress.com

FIRE SONG
PUBLISHED BY ENDURANCE PRESS
577 N Cardigan Ave
Star, ID 83669 U.S.A.

Bolding in Scripture quotations reflects the authors' added emphasis.

Cover photo's used by permission www.123rf.com

ISBN 978-0-9856746-0-1
eISBN 978-0-9856746-1-8

Cover Design by C Sarton Design
Author photo courtesy of BAMBoise.com
Printed in the United States of America
First Edition 2012

TABLE OF CONTENTS

FORWARD

Life is filled with moments. Some we love to remember and some we wish we could forget. But every once in awhile, a moment comes along that changes the course of our lives. Moments like these compel us to look back and say, "That's when it all started–that's when the transformation began."

For me that moment occurred at a hip little coffee shop in Tempe, AZ where I met John Mitchell. What started as a simple conversation turned into a 9-month journey, with John mentoring and guiding me into the greatest truth I know: Jesus Christ.

Looking back, I am utterly blown away by God's perfection. He knew just the person I needed and the perfect time to bring that person into my life. Not only was John an extremely gifted theologian and apologist (I drilled him with every question in the book), he was and is an amazing man, great father and husband, and business man. In meeting John, I met someone about whom I could honestly say, "If I turned out like him, my life would be a success."

FORWARD

John has an extraordinary ability to relate the story of the Gospel in a way that makes it understandable and applicable to one's life. His ability is on full display here as he takes us on a journey of the mind and spirit, in pursuit of the melody that resonates deep within our souls.

Fire Song is an amazing, powerful, and insightful book. As you read it, I hope and pray you encounter one of those "moments" I experienced with John at the coffee shop.

– Johnny Meier
Filmmaker

ACKNOWLEDGEMENTS

Words cannot express my love and appreciation for my wife, Debbie. She is my closest ally, partner and friend. She models Jesus-like humility, love and mercy, and inspires me to follow in His steps more closely each day. I love you Debbie.

In the same way, I count it the highest privilege to be the father of our six children, some of whom are already adults. Thank you David, Rebecca, Karis, Jenna, Melissa and Trea for sharing your lives with me - for your willingness to laugh at my tired jokes, and your patience with an eccentric, nerd of a dad.

Life is relationships. I am grateful for the deep and lasting friendships I enjoy with Johnny Meier, Dave Stone and Chris Bonga. These men have not only encouraged me in this project from the beginning, but they constantly challenge me to dream big and never settle. Here's to advancing God's Kingdom on the edges, men!

I am also indebted to my friends, Scott Duncan and Chris Mitchell for encouraging me to write. And *Fire Song* would not be what it is without friends who became gracious and tenacious reviewers, including my wife Debbie, Brad Kline,

Dawn Grove and David Hegg.

Recognizing that none of us are who we are, apart from the deposits of others, I am grateful for the intellectual mentoring of my friend, JP Moreland, along with the patient training of Doug Geivett, Scott Rae and others. In addition, as the astute reader will see, I am indebted to the works of C.S. Lewis, N.T. Wright, Tim Keller, William Lane Craig and many others.

I want to thank Jon Strain for his long friendship, and for connecting me with Endurance Press.

Most of all, I owe my life to the One who found me and taught me to sing again with Him. My highest aim is to make you famous, Jesus. Thank you for showing me how to live life wide awake.

– John A. Mitchell

Introduction:

A Handprint on the Wall

It was a prized possession that was all about me. A handprint in a pie-tin plaster mold. Important to me because my hand made that impression, complete with five-year-old fingerprints that were uniquely mine. Remember pressing your hand into a plaster mold, or maybe wet cement? And how proud you were for creating this enduring monument to your existence?

As I grew, I would measure my hand against that mold to assure myself I was growing. Seven years later, I was a fun loving, curious twelve-year old, hunting tadpoles, smashing rocks and walking the fields of our small Idaho farm. I remember, even then, pondering the nature of life. I wondered if I was the only real human being on Planet Earth. Was I surrounded by robot-humans and being studied by aliens? Were there other worlds? Why was I here? Did my handprint matter?

During this time of wondering, I lost hope in organized religion, which had begun to feel like an irrelevant game to me. Though I attended church regularly with my family, I increasingly felt as though it had no bearing on my life.

This intuition was cemented in my mind one Sunday morning when I approached the priest with a spiritual question. Instead of taking me or my question seriously, he smiled, patted me on the head and went on his way. Whether he thought my question did not matter, or he simply had no answer, his silence screamed in my ears. Religion could not explain my world after all. But I longed to understand the story I found myself in, and especially my place within it.

.....

Anthropologists recently discovered a prehistoric cave containing remnants of a people who lived many thousands of years ago. The scientists' most stunning find was not an artifact, but a well preserved work of art—a colorful outline of a handprint "spray painted" on the cave wall. An ancient artist, it seems, mixed pigment and saliva in his mouth, pressed his hand against the wall, and blew red "paint" around the edges of his hand and fingers. The clear and beautiful handprint that remained left a testimony to this person's creativity and self-expression.

Gazing at this ancient work of art, the handprint seems eerily familiar to me. Somehow, I feel connected to the one who so thoughtfully left his mark on history. I cannot help but wonder what he was thinking as he stepped back to enjoy his creation, the proof that he'd been there.

Did he take his friends to the cave now and then to show them *his* handprint? Did he declare, as we might, "this is *my* handprint," convinced it was significant because it was his? Did he think of us wondering about him? If so, what would he want us to know about him? What did he think about himself? Perhaps he simply desired what I did. What you did, as you proudly pressed your hand into that plaster mold or wet cement, carefully carving your name and the date in what would become a time capsule of your existence.

These moments of self-expression often come with as many questions as they do feelings of pride. We have this in common with our ancient friend. Like you and me, his artwork likely reflected a yearning to find his place in history and mark his presence there; to say, "I am here, even though I'm not completely sure who I am or what the point of life is." Somehow, self-expression helps us discover what it means to be us.

This quest for meaning is common to every culture, and invariably leads to answers in the form of stories, which become over-arching narratives that shape our self-understanding, define our place in the world, and attempt to connect us to the ancient drama that brings us all together.

What is this epic tale that unites and defines us as human beings? Somehow, we know the opening act of this play predates our kind, that our entrance onto the stage points to something bigger than ourselves. But we also believe we play a vital role in this unfolding saga and somehow shape its script.

Ironically, and unfortunately, most of us feel disconnected from the ancient story, as if we've been set adrift and don't know the way home. But we retain a memory, however faint, of the way we were and ought to be, but no longer are. Like the echo of a melody we never learned but once knew by heart, the ancient story beckons us to sing again.

Unlike memories of facts and places that come and go without consequence, the memory of this song burns deeply within us, bringing passion, meaning and definition to our lives. But it's as faded as it is deep. We remember, as in a dream, celebrating the melody with others in a symphony filled with life. We long to sing again, but we can't quite remember the tune.

And yet, even the echo of this song shapes our deepest intuitions and yearnings. All our pursuits in life reflect our desire to rediscover the ancient melody and find our place in its chorus. The purpose of this book is to help us remember the song we once knew and sing it together again; to uncover the ancient story it tells and find our place in it; to make sense of our handprint on the wall.

You'll find as we move forward that I believe the best story wins—not the most creative or clever story, but the one that most fully accounts for and explains our core intuitions and experiences in life. I believe the ancient story of Jesus uniquely accomplishes this. Jesus claimed that He alone brings all the notes together so we can sing again. However, my goal is not to debate this point until you believe as I do. Instead, I hope to invoke your intuitions as I invite you to trace your origins to the ancient drama that is our story.

We're all in different places on our journeys. I welcome you to begin where you are and journey forward with me—not by asking complicated questions that take us down rabbit holes with no end, but by asking obvious questions which lead to common-sense, intuitive answers that remind us of what we've always known.

To make this experience more personal, I've added *toggles* throughout the book. These are like footnotes, only better, as they give you the option to explore an idea in the book more fully. The topic of each toggle appears in a box in the right margin next to the relevant text. Follow toggles to the end of the chapters, if you wish, or ignore them and keep reading. You can enjoy the entire book without looking at a single toggle. Or you can pour over each one in detail.

I invite you, now, to turn the page and let the music begin.

Chapter One

Fire in the Equation

I needed a break in my routine, so I drove to a coffee shop to get some work done. I hadn't been there long when I began chatting with—get this—a rocket scientist, a bona-fide astrophysicist.

Somewhere in the conversation, I mentioned I was a follower of Jesus and a pastor, and I asked about his work. When I learned he trafficked in theoretical physics, I, naturally, asked if he was a Star Trek fan.

He was! Who would have guessed?

So I pulled out my pocket protector, hiked up my pants, and began talking Spock, the Starship Enterprise, and getting beamed around by the famed Star Trek transporter. To my delight, my new friend explained the physics behind the transporter concept and why it was theoretically possible to beam people through space.

Not to be out-geeked, I told him I had thought a lot about this (sadly, I really had), and I believed it was impossible for human persons to be broken into bits and beamed around the universe. In fact, I suggested, contrary to the notion that human beings are purely physical, the transporter concept proves that, at our core, we are immaterial beings (souls) that live in and through our physical bodies. Check out the toggle to get a taste of how that part of our conversation went. It was a blast.

Though my new friend was intrigued by my argument for the existence of the soul, he held his ground and insisted that things like non-physical souls don't exist. The rest of our conversation went something like this...

"All that exists is physical," he declared. "Eventually, science will explain everything."

"Wow," I replied. "Then you will never be able to account for the most basic and wonderful things in life!"

Obviously surprised, he asked what I meant.

"Think about love. Can you fill a test tube with a mother's love for her child? Can you point to love on the periodic table? Or express its power in a mathematical formula? Of course not. But love is just as real and at least as profound as all these things. Few people are expert scientists, like yourself, but even a small child recognizes the mysterious beauty of love."

The Star Trek Transporter Points to the Soul!

With a thoughtful shrug, he seemed to say, "as difficult as it is to explain things like love, they somehow make sense in a purely physical universe."

I continued. "If everything is purely physical, how do you account for good and evil, right and wrong? Atoms and sub-atomic particles are just rapidly moving pieces of stuff randomly bumping into each other. If, as you claim, all we are are bundles of these particles, why is it *good* to help an old lady across the street but *bad* to hit her over the head with her umbrella?

How is the collision between the umbrella and her head morally different than two stones colliding randomly on a mountain in Yemen? How come one cluster of colliding particles has value, but the other doesn't? You need to add something to the physical realm in order to speak meaningfully of values, of good and evil."

My new friend appeared intrigued, or at least amused, so I continued. "If all we are is physical stuff, and our brains are the product of purely physical, and therefore, *non*-rational, random collisions between pieces of matter over time, how can you be confident the collisions in your brain lead to rational conclusions about the world? How can you claim to *know* anything at all, if the basis of your knowledge flows from random, non-rational forces?"

"But we clearly do know things," I said. "For example, I know I'm a *person* who loves and recognizes goodness and pursues justice. I also know I am more than my body. Though the physical parts of my body and brain are constantly changing or dying, the core *me* remains the same person (an unbroken stream of consciousness) who exists through these changes.

I am the actual self who learned to ride a bike when I was four, and I will be the identical self who struggles to get on a bike when I'm ninety-four. My absolute identity through physical change means *I* am more than my ever-changing body. This *more than my body* is what many call the soul."

The scientist chuckled. "You are a very strange pastor. I'm not used to hearing Christians talk like this."

We both laughed.

And then he said, "These are interesting questions I must wrestle with, even though we scientists try not to get caught up in religious debates. We call mysteries such as this the *fire in the equation*—that part of reality our theories can't explain."

Ah, I thought to myself, even scientists must walk by faith.

Then I asked him, "Why not just live in the fire? If the best things in life are found in-between your theories, I want to live there, don't you?"

He didn't respond, but I could tell his mental wheels were spinning at high speed as we said our goodbyes and went our separate ways.

This encounter reminded me that the stories told by the physical sciences fill in some important blanks about who we are. But, as my new friend began to see, a purely physical view of the world cannot explain our deepest and most valued intuitions about what it means to be human.

Surely the ancient story we find ourselves in must answer the biggest questions of life and account for the passions, dreams and desires that burn within us. Dogmatically asserting a view of the world that can't account for these things is foolish at best, sub-human at worst.

To be fair, many scientists believe in something more than what they can measure in physical terms. Many believe in the immaterial world, souls and God. They understand that experiencing the fullness of life means embracing the fire in the equation.

But if the stories told by physics are incomplete, what is the rest of the story? Where does the fire come from? Compelled to make sense of it all, various storytellers have tried to bring the pieces together in various ways. In what follows, we will listen to and examine ancient stories that claim to explain what it means to be human. Some take us closer to the fire than others. But only one story ignites our full humanity, sets our hearts ablaze, and teaches us to sing again.

The Star Trek Transporter Points to the Soul!

According to my friend, the theory behind the Star Trek transporter is simple. First, a computer maps every cell in the body of the traveler who is to be beamed up or down. Next, the transporter mechanism disassembles the body of the traveler by breaking it into billions of tiny pieces of matter. Finally, these particles are reassembled in the new location, according to the detailed map of the traveler's body that was stored in the computer's memory. The new body is reconstructed using matter from the original body, in addition to matter it mixes with in the process.

After this explanation, I asked my friend where the traveler goes during his or her "transport." "It seems clear to me," I said, "that a person would cease to exist (die) when his or her body was broken into billions of pieces."

"Ah, but an exact replica of that person is assembled in the new location," he insisted, "complete with an identical body and brain, containing the identical memories of the person who had been disassembled by the transporter."

"But an exact replica of something isn't the same as the thing replicated," I said. "The clone of a thing isn't the thing itself. The person who ceases to exist at the beginning of 'transport' is not the same person who is assembled from a map of that person's body stored in a computer."

"I can prove this to you," I said. "What if the transporter took the information about the person's body and brain and, instead of assembling only one replica of the original person, it produced three identical replicas of the traveler from surrounding matter. Suppose each of these replicas was constructed simultaneously, from precisely the same amount of matter from the original body, mixed in with additional matter from the surrounding area. Finally, assume each replica of the traveler was assembled and experienced consciousness simultaneously in the new location. Who would count as the original traveler who was transported, and how would you know?"

My friend looked puzzled. I knew he couldn't answer this question decisively because his criterion for identifying the traveler was the traveler's body/brain map saved in the computer. But this, obviously, is not enough to identify the traveler, because this map could have multiple, identical people embodying it.

Our thought experiment with the transporter reveals at least two things. First, the only way for a person to actually travel through space and time is for that person to endure the journey as a single entity, with a single, uninterrupted stream of mental, emotional and volitional capacity (personhood) through every stage of the journey. Because the traveler's personhood would be destroyed when his body and brain were obliterated by the machine, he would cease to exist at the beginning of the journey. The one who replaced him would not be him—just one who perfectly resembled him. This means the original traveler would not, in any sense, be transported to another place by the machine.

Second, to say a person maintains his or her absolute identity through physical change assumes that he or she is more than just physical parts. For if a person is identical to the set of physical parts that make up his or her body and brain, then no actual person would endure through body/brain change, only "person-stages" that sequentially replace one another.

Think about it. Our bodies and brains change radically over time, gaining and losing billions of cells or other components almost daily. But if I am identical to a certain set of body and brain parts, when that set of parts is replaced by a different set (i.e., when my body and brain change), then "I," by definition, would cease to exist in that moment, and a similar "person-stage" would replace "me." No literal self would make the journey through these physical changes, unless the self is more than physical parts.

This matches my intuitions perfectly. I know that I am a single entity who's gone through radical changes while remaining identical to myself. What about you? My guess is you know without a doubt that you are literally the same person who enrolled in kindergarten and made an imprint of your hand in plaster. You are the same, single entity, who has grown and changed through time.

Your body and brain have gained and lost billions of cells throughout your lifetime. And yet, you, an enduring entity with a single stream of uninterrupted mental, emotional and volitional capacity have remained the same person throughout these changes. But for this to be true, you must be more than your physical parts. You must be a non-physical soul that exists in and through a physical body. Your "soulishness" is what makes you a person.

Chapter Two

Storytellers East of Jersey

They fit the "young film-maker" stereotype perfectly. High-energy, creatively rebellious, and exuding confidence that their next movie would rock the world.

I met Johnny and Dave at the *Extreme Bean* coffee shop in Tempe, Arizona. Dave was in his late twenties and Johnny was close behind. When I first saw them, they were engaged in an intense phone conversation. Dave was on the call and Johnny was listening carefully.

Turns out, Dave was firing a director who had botched their current film. As the call came to an end, the two of them began to review the situation. I slipped into the conversation by asking if everything was all right.

After explaining the issue regarding their director, we began talking about film, the arts and our common desire to influence culture. At some point, I mentioned I was a follower of Jesus, whom I believed was the greatest cultural revolutionary in history. That comment launched a discussion that would take us deep into friendship and ongoing conversation about life.

We began meeting weekly at the *Bean* and at a local pub. As our relationships grew, I learned that Johnny had been on a spiritual quest for some time. Like many in his generation, he was intrigued by stories from the Far East, and was pursuing a popular form of Buddhism.

Johnny later told me he'd hoped my talk of Jesus would make him a better Buddhist. He knew all about the fire, and he wanted to feel the burn. Dave wasn't quite as interested at first. But he was very bright, and they both asked challenging questions.

Over the next several weeks, we agreed to search for the story that connects the puzzle pieces of life, and satisfies our most treasured intuitions and aspirations as human beings.

This meant we would talk about things like *personal identity* - how we are individual selves who endure through change, who think, feel and act.

We would also discuss our profound need for *relationships* with people, nature, and, perhaps, God, as well as our unquenchable desire to connect with a *purpose* greater than ourselves.

We would address the undeniable existence of *good and evil*, and the mystery of *beauty*. We also wanted to address our desire for *justice* in the world, since we agreed that things on earth are not what they should be.

As we explored how various stories satisfied or fell short of meeting our intuitions, we agreed that the physical sciences reveal important parts of our story, but cannot explain things like purpose and dreams, good and evil, beauty, love, souls or spirituality. Johnny had been chasing these things through Buddhism, an increasingly appealing philosophy in Western culture that originally grew out of ancient Hinduism.

Buddhism?
Hinduism?

While the Hindu and Buddhist stories of the world are different, their core beliefs are similar and lead to the same practical conclusions about life. For example, both reject absolute distinctions between things, because only one thing exists. Hinduism calls the one thing *God* or *Brahman*, the impersonal, all-consuming "what is" that lives in and expresses itself *as* the universe. For the Hindu, everything that exists is an emanation or expression of Brahman.

Agreeing with Hinduism that only one thing exists, Buddhism teaches that the One is *not* God. It's simply the non-personal "everything that is." So Hinduism and Buddhism take us in the same basic direction. Both insist that because only the One (or Brahman) exists, all perceived distinctions in the world, like hot and cold, individual people, good and evil, or freedom and bondage, are mere illusions. No wonder both Hinduism and Buddhism see the goal of life as shedding one's personal identity, choosing to believe we're not individuals after all, but mere drops in the ocean of the One or Brahman.

I detail similarities and differences between these two stories in a toggle. For now, because Buddhism was Johnny's focus, let's consider the practical implications of the story Buddhism tells and talk about Hinduism along the way.

As we learned about Buddhism together, Johnny, Dave and I wrestled with the idea of the *One*.

We began by trying to make sense of the idea that distinctions do not exist, that good and evil, persons, relationships, colors and tastes are just imaginary—residing in individual minds which don't exist either. After all, say our Buddhist friends, only the One exists, but not really. It too defies any category of being.

Do these ideas seem difficult to follow? Don't worry. Buddhism rejects logic and reason as well, insisting the way to enlightenment is to let go of analysis, the desire to know, and, ultimately, the idea that you are a self. The goal of life is simply to *be* in the present moment. Of course, neither moments nor selves exist, so being in the moment is an illusion as well.

Have you ever heard of karma? This Hindu, then Buddhist concept is at the heart of these Eastern stories. Karma is basically the law of consequences associated with action, and roughly equivalent to positive or negative energy attached to good or bad deeds. According to Hinduism and Buddhism, a person accumulates good karma by doing good deeds and sheds bad karma through suffering.

The more good karma one stores up, the closer that person is to attaining "nirvana," a word that means, to extinguish, blow out, or cease to exist. To achieve nirvana is to stop thinking, feeling and desiring as an individual. When *I*, a single drop of water blend into the ocean of the One (Brahman for the Hindu), nirvana takes place.

If an individual lacks enough good karma to do nirvana at the end of his life, he must go through another life, or another hundred-thousand lives, until he gets it right. This striving for perfection is the basis for the high ethical standards in Buddhism and Hinduism, though it is difficult to understand why, if, as both claim, neither good nor evil, nor persons to do good or evil actually exist. But if you don't push it too far, the appeal of Buddhism is clear.

How convenient to be released from the rigors of reason, and annoying realities like right and wrong. Since good and evil are illusions, the Buddhist eventually comes to the place of no longer concerning himself with these distinctions, or any other form of judgement. And with the removal of judgment comes the removal of responsibility.

All I must do is *be* as I am, in the moment I find myself, as part of the One.

Buddhism is also attractive because it teaches the deep unity of all things, matching our intuition that we are somehow connected to one another.

In addition, this ancient story offers a way to eradicate evil, by eliminating all desires (and the "individuals" who have desires) since, according to Buddhism, desires lead to disappointment, which leads to suffering. And suffering is the essence of evil.

Johnny was attracted to many of these Buddhist teachings, but he hadn't considered where they were leading him. In time, I asked if the story he'd been following fueled the fire in his soul. Did it meet his deep intuitions about his identity as a person? His relationship to others? His desire for purpose?

Did Buddhism satisfy his intuitions about good and evil, beauty, or his desire for justice and social transformation? Point by point, we concluded that we had to deny too many of our dearest intuitions to embrace this story and others like it.

Denying the existence of good and evil is staggering in itself. I cannot view evil as an illusion any more than I can pretend that I am an illusion. Buddhism and Hinduism ask us to do both.

And while the idea of karma may seem cool to some in the West, truth be told, *karma sucks*. If you're like me, it would take an infinite number of life cycles to rid yourself of bad karma and gain enough good karma to do nirvana (know anyone who is even close?).

And here's another problem: If karma is real, we should never help anyone who is suffering. Why? Because, by easing their pain, we would interrupt the purging of their bad karma. In other words, helping those who are suffering is the most selfish thing I can do, because I earn good karma by keeping them from shedding bad karma through their suffering. Something is deeply wrong with this picture.

Johnny and I had a mutual Buddhist friend who struggled with this aspect of karma. But he insisted we shouldn't press the logic too far. Such questions must not be asked, our friend said, because they lead to mental angst and suffering, which is evil.

But that was an unsatisfying response, even for Johnny. Evaluating the foundations of a story that claims to put the pieces of life together is *precisely* what we must do to understand where that story takes us. But the closer Dave, Johnny and I looked, the more we saw that these stories from the East ask us to deny too many of our core intuitions, like personal identity.

Buddhism (and Hinduism) tell me I'm not really a self; that distinctions between persons are imaginary. *I* am an illusion and so are *you*. The sooner *I* understand this, the sooner I achieve nirvana.

Many think "nirvana" is just another word for heaven, a place where individuals experience ecstasy forever. But in nirvana, no individuals exist to experience anything, because, by definition, all individuals, along with their desires, have been blown out like candles in the wind. In other words, nirvana is the ultimate *non-experience* that results when the illusion of self is finally extinguished.

But to say my experience as *me* is just an illusion violates my deep intuition that I am an individual being who longs to live a meaningful life today, and exist forever as the *me* that I am. My deepest yearning isn't to be blown out. I want to burn brightly together with others for something bigger than myself, today and forever. I want to advance meaningful causes and pursue important goals. But if *I* don't actually exist, then *I* can't make meaningful decisions of any kind—which, on a personal note, means I couldn't have accepted my friend's challenge to shoot him in the rear-end with a pellet gun when we were kids.

Actually, we were sixteen-years old and in high school. I was hanging out at Rick's house and we were shooting his pellet gun. It was a classic, air-driven, pump-in-the-stock gun that fired individually loaded pellets.

I had grown up shooting pellet guns like this one at snakes, cans, and various critters around our place. Rick didn't realize this when he challenged me to take a shot at him. "Go ahead," he yelled, as he trotted forty yards down the street, bent over and laughed. "See if you can hit me."

As he ran, I pumped the pellet gun again and again and again, pressing as much pressure into the chamber as possible. This would be a tough shot. Taking aim at the left rear pocket of his blue jeans, I lifted the barrel about an inch to account for distance and squeezed the trigger.

Rick leaped into the air and let out a scream I'm sure still reverberates over Meridian, Idaho. "You hit me," he wailed, as he dropped his pants to examine an impressive and growing welt on the upper back of his leg. Thirty years later, we're still laughing about that lucky shot.

Now, I'm not suggesting Rick or I made a good decision that day. But I am saying we were able to make this and other (hopefully more productive) decisions because we aren't just illusions. We are actually existing selves.

How strange we even have to make this point. Yet, if individual people don't really exist (as Buddhism insists), the trouble goes even deeper. For example, if these Eastern stories are true, then love is impossible, not only because love is itself an illusion, but because no actual persons exist to love or be loved.

Johnny once introduced me to one of his Buddhist mentors, Martin. A fun-loving, delightful Jamaican, Martin often spoke with joy of his young son whom he loved very much. One night, my wife asked if Martin understood that, according to his belief system, the relationship he enjoyed with his son wasn't even real. In fact, his son wasn't real. Did he understand that his love for his boy was an illusion, as was his son's love for him? Did he grasp that moving toward nirvana meant "blowing out" his desire to love and be loved by his son?

If the story we claim doesn't make room for our most basic and wonderful desires, can it be the true story we are searching for? I think not, especially when we compare this story to the life and story of Jesus, who said that the highest expression of humanity is to be a redeemed (healed) person in right relationship with God and others. Buddhism, on the other hand, insists that our highest aspiration should be to cease loving, caring, feeling and relating.

To be fair, the Buddhist is correct in asserting that, as more and more people move toward nirvana, there would be less and less suffering in the world. But this is only because no selves would exist to do evil (or good). Consider an example.

Let's say my Pontiac has a steering problem, so I take it to the mechanic and say, "Something is wrong with the steering. I don't want to drive it like this anymore."

"Hmm," the mechanic replies. "So you don't want a car with poor steering. That is a problem. Guess we'll have to blow up the whole thing. Then you'll no longer have a car that runs badly."

On the one hand, the mechanic would be correct. My problem would be solved by destroying the car. On the other hand—well, you see the other hand. But this is precisely what Buddhism and Hinduism ask us to do to solve the problem of evil.

They rightly admit the brokenness of man and the world.

But snuffing out the broken people is not the same as redeeming, healing or fixing them. I am a broken self, to be sure. But I long for redemption, not the blowing out or blowing up of my personhood.

I'm sure you're getting the picture. Like a purely physical explanation of the universe, the big stories from the East leave us wanting more. So our search continues for a story that accounts for the fact we live in a personal—not an impersonal—universe, populated with personal beings who love, choose, create, dream and enjoy distinctions.

It's in *this* universe where the fire burns brightly and ignites in us a song that reminds us who we are and what it means to be human.

Hinduism? Buddhism?

Hinduism and Buddhism are closely related in origin and foundational beliefs. Hinduism came first, appearing on the Indian subcontinent around 2000 B.C., perhaps earlier. Hinduism does not have a founder, per se, but the oldest of the sacred Hindu texts, known as the Vedas, date to approximately 1400 B.C. The Upanishads came next, between 700 and 300 B.C., followed by the Mahabharata and the Bhagavad Gita.* While other sacred Hindu texts exist, these are among the most read and revered.

Buddhism was founded by a Hindu named Siddhartha Gautama, a wealthy prince from the Brahmin (priestly) caste, in what is known today as Nepal, in sixth-century B.C. Much of his life is shrouded in myth and legend, but it seems that in his late 20s, Siddhartha became acutely aware of and deeply disturbed by suffering and death in the world. Dissatisfied with the Hindu explanation for evil, he left his wealth and power to seek an end to suffering and death.

In the process of rigid asceticism and meditation, he believed he came to a new realization or enlightenment regarding how to end the cycle of suffering and death that dominates our world. Thus, he became known as "Buddha," which means "awake one" or "enlightened one." His new philosophy was deeply rooted in the basic tenets of Hinduism, but with some important differences.

The complexities of these belief systems cannot be explained fully here. However, for those who are interested, I encourage you to investigate Hindu and Buddhist texts and resources to get a handle on the details. For now, let me expand upon and clarify some of the main points I discuss in this chapter. I will elucidate similarities and important differences between these two systems, as they speak to the issues of God, the soul and salvation.

You may want to examine and evaluate this summary with your own research. The following websites will get you started: uwacadweb.uwyo.edu/religionet/er/hinduism/htexts.htm and www.bbc.co.uk/religion/religions/.

God

Hinduism is thoroughly *monistic*, insisting that only one thing ultimately exists—Brahman (God).

But Brahman is not a personal being. Nor does he create others who are separate from his essential being. Brahman is impersonal, or beyond personal, and everything that exists is merely an expression or emanation of Brahman, who is all things.

Some have mistakenly called Hindu theology pantheistic. It is more accurate to call it panentheistic. Even though all "things" (individual existents) are emanations of God, and He exists in, through and as all things, God is somehow more than His potentially infinite emanations.

Hindu monism and panentheistic theology provide the foundation for Hinduism. For example, since only God exists, individual souls (persons) are an illusion. Because we are all just part of Brahman, no true individuals exist. Hindu theology insists that we and everything in the universe is/are Brahman.

Siddhartha Gautama (Buddha) held firmly to the monism of Hinduism, but rejected its theology. Thus, in Buddhism, there is no God, only the "One." And the One is completely beyond comprehension, analysis, being or nonbeing. The One neither exists nor doesn't exist. This is very difficult to understand. But this "middle way" between being and non-being is foundational to Buddhism.

As with Hindu theology, Buddhist non-theology has profound ramifications for human beings. Specifically, as we will see, because the One has no category of being, and since "we" are all "part" of the One, we have no category of being either. We neither exist nor don't exist. Thus, holding to the self as absolute in any way must be rejected.

Our non-existence lays the groundwork for the Buddhist belief that "nirvana" means ceasing to exist as a thinking, feeling, pursuing individual. More accurately, nirvana is not a state-of-being at all, because it involves the recognition that one never exists as an individual person.

The Soul

Hinduism affirms the existence of human souls. More specifically, Brahman emanates the divine essence into illusory individual souls called Atman. Since only Brahman exists, Hinduism boldly declares that Atman is Brahman. In other words, souls exist, but souls are not independent existents or persons. They are merely modes or expressions of Brahman, who alone exists. Thus, according to Hinduism, our perception that our soul (personal identity) is absolute or independent from Brahman is merely an illusion.

The illusory self plays a key role in the Hindu version of salvation, which calls us to recognize and admit that we are not individuals after all. We are less than drops in the ocean of Brahman, who alone exists.

Buddhism rejects the existence of the soul altogether. No God exists. No souls (individual people) exist. Only the One exists, but not really. Siddhartha Gautama (Buddha) used the word "anatta," which means, "no Atman" to describe this view. Together with the rejection of God, the rejection of the soul (individual) plays a key role in the Buddhist view of salvation, since the non-existence of the soul makes it truly possible to stop the cycle of life, death and rebirth by finally "entering" the realm of not existing as a person.

Salvation

Hindu and Buddhist salvation include the ideas of karma, samsara, and nirvana (Buddhism) or moksha (Hinduism). Karma is essentially cause-and-effect associated with good or bad deeds that bring positive or negative consequences into the salvation journey of the "individual." Samsara refers to the transmigration (reincarnation) of the soul as part of the ongoing cycle of redemptive birth, death, and rebirth, as individuals work out the bad karma and store up enough good karma to reach nirvana or moksha.

Moksha (Hindu salvation) is defined as breaking free from the hierarchical caste system and losing oneself (literally) in the ocean of Brahman's being. This takes place for the Hindu as he reincarnates from the lower to higher social castes, until he finally enters the Brahmin (priestly) caste and, when he has enough good karma, is able to leave the process and un-differentiate into the being of Brahman.

Though the individual no longer "exists" in moksha, there is perfection in the being of Brahman, of which the emanation that was "you" was a part. Not surprisingly, Hindus differ on how moksha works and what this "experience" is like for the non-existent individual in this state.

In Buddhism, nirvana, which means "to extinguish" or "blow out," is much like moksha, except nirvana is available to all people in every caste. Once achieved, nirvana ultimately means ceasing to exist altogether. Though similar to Hindu moksha in this regard, Buddhism is even stronger in insisting that the soul, which never existed in any sense, certainly does not exist in nirvana. This is how the cycle of suffering and death is finally and truly broken—by removing all sentience (passion, feeling, desire, etc.) from the universe.

* "Sacred Texts and Traditional Tales." "Hinduism." Exploring Religions. Aug 2012 uwacadweb.uwyo.edu/religionet/er/hinduism/htexts.htm

Chapter Three

Chocolate-Covered Strawberries

To say she has an obsession would be an understatement. The transformation is swift and stark when my daughter Melissa sees a chocolate-covered strawberry. Her eyes glaze over and her jaw drops open. She loses track of her surroundings and she begins to drool. I think I heard a low growl the last time I approached her while she was eating her favorite treat.

As for me, I can take or leave chocolate-covered strawberries, but coat a piece of toffee with chocolate, or place a slice of my wife's lasagna in front of me, and I join Melissa in taste-bud paradise.

I have the same experience when I sip a Kilt Lifter, "*an ale made in the tradition of the great strong ales of Scotland. Amber colored, malty sweet, with an underlying note of smokiness.*"[1] Mmmm. Even the description makes my mouth water.

---

1 From the menu at Four Peaks Brewery, Tempe, AZ

You Taste
with Your
Soul

What about you? What tasty treat do you crave? Ben and Jerry's ice cream? Deep-dish pizza? Sushi rolls or a fresh green salad? Hot buttered popcorn, a crisp cool apple, or fresh corn on the cob?

Have you ever wondered why food tastes so good? Certainly we could survive without flavors, taste buds and treats. So why are they a part of life? And why are we made to enjoy them? What, if anything, do they suggest about the nature of our world and our purpose as human beings?

Could it be we were meant to encounter, taste, and relish life, not merely endure it? This intuition intensifies when a man gazes at the beauty of a woman, when we breathe the scent of a pine forest, or take a cool swim in the heat of summer. We're awestruck by the canvas of a sunset, the majesty of the ocean, or the magnificence of lightning against a blackened sky. We experience delight when we blow soap bubbles from a wand, catch snowflakes on our tongues, enjoy faithful middle C, or watch puppies play.

Have you felt the mysterious power of romance, studied a picture of a distant galaxy, or marveled at the simple complexity of a DNA molecule? We're surrounded by indescribable beauty, countless pleasures and endless delights. And we're made to enjoy them! This tells us something important about who we are, why we're here, and who's behind our universe.

As we reflect on the characteristics that define our world, it's fair to ask, "In what kind of universe would we expect to find such things?" For example, does the existence of beauty (and our ability to enjoy it) seem more at home in an impersonal, random universe, or in one that is inherently personal and purposeful? Do your vivid encounters with the sights, tastes, sounds and scents of this world suggest you live in a universe where these things are mere illusions? Or are they something more?

The answers to these questions give us clues that lead us ever closer to the ancient story that defines us. In addition to things like beauty and pleasure, I'm convinced the existence of good and evil, love and relationships, purposeful desires, even humor, point to the personal fabric of our universe, which implies a personality behind our universe. Let me show you what I mean.

The reality of good and evil

Do moral laws exist? Or is morality defined by the individual? What makes one action right but another wrong? Is morality just a way of saying we *prefer* some actions over others? Or are some acts inherently wrong because they violate moral principles that define us as human beings?

Is the tribe that deliberately tortures and kills its young morally equal to one that protects and honors all its people? Is the act of helping your grandmother cross a busy street in the rain morally equivalent to throwing a lasso around her neck and dragging her behind your car?

While some aspects of morality depend on the circumstances, eventually we all agree that some actions are morally right, while others are simply wrong.

Few deny Hitler was morally wrong to systematically torture and slaughter millions of human beings just to build his empire. And most believe Mother Teresa's acts of kindness toward the dying poor were beautiful *because* they were morally good. It is intuitively obvious that rape, abuse and using people as a means to self-centered ends is morally repugnant. But sacrificing comfort to protect the vulnerable, speak for the voiceless, and stand for the oppressed is morally good and inspirational.

Though moral dilemmas exist, and sometimes right and wrong blur on the edges of the page, generally speaking, we recognize goodness when we see it. And, eventually, we all appeal to some form of absolute goodness or morality, usually when we feel like *our* moral rights have been violated.

But why is this? Why do we share this sense of the way things ought to be, not only for ourselves but for others as well? Why do we cringe when people suffer at the hands of a tyrant and cheer when the tyrant falls? Why do we scorn the child abuser and feel compelled to help his victim recover from his evil against her? Why do we long for peace on earth, the end of war and crime, and unity among all people?

And more than simply desiring these things, how is it that deep down, we know this is how things were *meant* to be but no longer are.

This lack of how things ought to be is what most people call *evil*—the lack of good. If goodness were a donut, evil would be the hole in the middle (the lack of donut). If goodness is viewed as light, evil would be darkness (the absence of light). Evil is the absence or lack of what is good.

Strangely, some try to deny that absolute goodness exists by pointing to evil in the world. But doesn't calling something *evil* point to a *good* standard that's been violated? Where does this standard come from? Put differently, why is morality part of the fabric of our universe?

This question is difficult to answer if you believe that only physical stuff exists. How do you get values, good and evil, or right and wrong from a gigantic, impersonal bundle of tiny particles randomly slamming into each other? Some try to avoid this problem by insisting that morals are simply *there*. Like atoms, hiccups and woodchucks, morality is just part of the universe's furniture.

But as soon as someone claims that morality is part of our universe, they're no longer acting as scientists but as philosophers, because the physical sciences have no category for things like values or right and wrong. Not only that, because morality applies to *persons*, not things, claiming the existence of morals in an *im*personal universe is incoherent. Once again, we see that the "physical stuff only" story fails to satisfy our deepest intuitions.

The major stories from the East don't fare any better, because they insist that good and evil are mere illusions in an impersonal universe.[2] While this view of morality might be consistent in an Eastern religious system, can anyone really live as if good and evil are less than real? Try convincing a rape victim the violence perpetrated against her wasn't really evil—or the orphans of Darfur that genocide is morally neutral.

We cannot deny that goodness is somehow part of the fabric of how things are meant to be. And it is painfully clear that ugly holes exist in this fabric. These holes are evil—the absence of good, that which is unlike the way things ought to be.

Some stories from the East, like Taoism (pronounced "dowism"), admit that good and evil are real, but then insist that both good and evil are *necessary* for proper balance in the universe. This view is sometimes referred to as "yin and yang," represented by a circular symbol that looks a bit like intertwined black-and-white tadpoles. You've

2 Hinduism tends to describe Brahman as beyond personal, rather than impersonal.

seen this symbol on advertisements for Chinese acupuncture—or maybe as a tattoo.

But, as cool as the symbol may look, it represents a view that fails our clearest intuitions. Specifically, I do *not* sense that evil is necessary. On the contrary, evil feels grossly out of place in the world. That's why we call it *wrong* and want to see evil conquered and replaced with goodness—the way things ought to be. The intensity of this intuition implies that it's a foundational component of our story, a key verse in the ancient song we long to sing again.

The Power of Love

I believe we know the most important things in life prior to reason or demonstration. For example, no one has to convince us of our desire to give and receive love or to be in relationship with others. Babies who don't receive tangible affection early in life develop attachment disorders that keep them from healthy relationships their entire lives. Premature babies who are held regularly in the hospital mature more quickly than those who receive only medical attention.

Being rejected by others is a universal human fear. This is why, even as adults, peer pressure is real and powerful. Something in us longs to connect with and be accepted by others, to be part of a community of people who accept us, love us, and allow us to love them in return.

We don't need anyone to convince us of these longings. They are part of us. We desire love for ourselves and rejoice when others experience it. We instinctively identify with and applaud the bond between mother and child—and celebrate a man and woman becoming husband and wife.

Brotherhood, sisterhood, fraternities, sororities, family reunions and birthday parties point to our innate desire to be connected with others, to love and be loved, to serve, protect and sacrifice for those we call our own.

Moms and dads the world over willingly lose sleep to make sure their babies are fed and safe. Friends sacrifice convenience to comfort one another in times of pain. Families stand together when crisis rocks their clan. Soldiers sacrifice their lives for each other in battle, and survivors wish they could have done the same for their comrades.

Relationships are so core to who we are, many of us would give our lives for the sake of those we love. But where does this deep devotion to others come from? And where does it point to? What does our universal longing for relationship and commitment to those we love reveal about the story we find ourselves in?

Some believe our world is the product of time plus chance and survival of the fittest. In this view, those who are best at *self*-preservation survive and reproduce others like themselves. People not as skilled at or devoted to *self*-preservation, we are told, don't survive or reproduce their kind as effectively. If this is true, why are loyalty, love and *self*-sacrifice so highly praised and such a dominant reality in the human experience? Don't these traits, by definition, threaten one's self-preservation?

Aware of this inconsistency, some insist that attributes like love, devotion and self-sacrifice are accidental byproducts of random evolutionary processes that now define us. But this idea is difficult to swallow, because it implies that the behaviors which make my life most beautiful and worth living are merely accidental. Really? Is this the best answer we can come up with? Again, we are compelled to ask—are persons who long to love and be loved more likely to be found in a random, impersonal universe, or a purposeful, personal universe; in a universe where persons are real or just an illusion?

The closer we look, the more difficult it becomes to deny that personality is woven into the very fabric of our universe, which strongly supports our deep intuition that personality lies behind our universe. Two more aspects of our world strengthen this conclusion even further.

Purposeful Pursuit

Have you ever set a goal, made a plan or had a dream? Maybe you set out to run a marathon, bike to work or lose a few pounds— and you did it. Why did your accomplishment feel so good?

Perhaps you've been part of a team that achieved a goal together. Why was this important to you?

Ever planted a garden and eaten the produce of your labor? No other vegetables ever tasted so good.

Have you started a new business, painted a landscape or captured a fleeting moment of beauty with a photo, poem or song? What is that feeling of satisfaction all about?

Why are we so pleased after we've served those in need or advanced a cause that makes a difference in our community? Why are we motivated to help the suffering, feed the hungry or offer hope to the hurting?

What kind of people continually look toward what might be? Why are we compelled to make life as it should be? What does this unending pursuit of purpose reveal about who we are and why we are here? In what kind of universe is the pursuit of purpose most likely to be found?

If we are descendants of purely random events and accidental mutations, is purpose even possible? If not, why do we yearn for it? Does our strong desire for purpose reveal a core intuition that our universe is laced with personal purpose to be pursued by purposeful people like you and me?

Interestingly, Jesus not only spoke of finding purpose in life, He continually invited His followers to enter ultimate purpose, calling them to pray,

"God, let your Kingdom come."[3] In other words, "Let me be about the business of building your Kingdom, God. Let your Kingdom be revealed in and through me."

Here, Jesus invites us to enter and advance what He sees as the greatest purpose possible—growing and revealing God's eternal Kingdom. All this bolsters our already strong sense that our universe is personal, and invites us to look for the personality behind it all.

Humor

I have a dog named Steve. He loves to ride in my car.

Whenever I pick up my keys or even put on my shoes, the little Maltese leaps into action and begs to go with me. On those occasions when I take him along, he eagerly leaps into the car, props himself on my lap and stretches his head out the window.

As we drive down the street, I swear he smiles as the wind blows back his dog-face fur. People driving the other direction sometimes point, smile or laugh. And who can blame them? Steve's antics

3 Matthew 6:10

are hilarious. So are otters having a water fight and hamsters running on a wheel. And just looking at a duck-billed platypus makes me chuckle.

People are funny, too. Have you ever wondered why we enjoy watching each other fall down or do foolish things? Or why laughter feels so good? Why is sarcasm so amusing and the Cartoon Network so popular?

No matter our station in life, humor has a way of finding us. Laughter is powerful medicine that can lower our blood pressure, strengthen our immune system and cause our bodies to release chemicals that promote a sense of well-being.

Why are humor, laughter and joy such important aspects of our lives? Again, we ask, in what sort of universe is humor most at home? In one that is wholly physical and mechanistic? Or in a personal and purposeful universe that science can't fully explain but reflects our deepest desires?

Does a world full of moral, loving, laughing persons who long to experience pleasure, beauty and purpose even make sense in an impersonal "Eastern" universe? Or do these things point to the inherently personal nature of all things, and beg us to pull back the curtain to meet the Personality behind it all?

Pointing to the *Book of Genesis*, the first book in the Bible, Jesus affirmed that before anything else existed, the personal God was there, and He created all things.[4] Jesus believed our beginning was purposeful, not accidental; personal, not mechanistic; and actual, not illusory. The story He told affirms what we know intuitively. And, as we'll see in Chapter Four, it also finds support in the nature of our universe, which had an absolute beginning that had to be caused by a choosing agent (person). To see why I'm convinced this is true, you must first try to imagine a truly empty canvas...

4 See, for example, Mark 10:6

You Taste With Your Soul

For a treat to be tasted, there must be a taster. For beauty to be enjoyed, there must be an enjoyer. Every experience requires an experiencer. Nothing too profound about that, right? But upon closer examination, it turns out that experiencers are the kind of thing that cannot be described in solely physical terms. Here's why:

Physical things do not and cannot have experiences. Rocks don't feel thirst, taste sugar or lose their appetite. Neither do cars, computers or carbon atoms. In the same way, a human-looking robot programmed to mimic a person tasting chocolate isn't really tasting anything, because tasting is more than a set of behaviors—it is a first-person encounter that an experiencer has with what he or she experiences. Since physical things do not and cannot have experiences, experiencers cannot be merely physical things.

Here's another way of looking at it. My experience is, by definition, my unique, first-person encounter which is unavailable to others. By way of contrast, everything about physical things is, at least in principle, available to third-person examination. For example, all that a carbon atom is and does is public information. But experiences are intrinsically private and available only to the experiencer. Since experiences are, by definition, first-person encounters that are inaccessible to the third-person observation that all physical things are subject to, experiences cannot be merely physical things.

Though we can approximate what others are experiencing because we believe we experience similar things and recognize their reactions, each person's experiences are inherently personal. I do not experience your pain, though I can relate to it because I have experienced pain. I cannot taste for you, though I can relate to your enjoyment of ice cream, because I have had first-person experiences with ice cream.

My experiences take place within me, where my memories, dreams, desires, pleasures, fears and pain reside. The holder of these thoughts and emotions is my soul, the non-physical (first-person) essence of who I am.

Chapter Four

The Color of Nothing

"Dad," my eleven-year-old Trea asked, "what color is nothing? Is it clear or just, like, white? Because that would be something, not nothing."

Trying to imagine reality before the universe came to be, Trea struggled to picture what *nothing* was like. But, of course, as she began to understand, nothing isn't *like* anything, because it's, well, *nothing*. Trying to imagine nothing is like trying to imagine a new primary color. We cannot do it because all we know is the realm of red, yellow and blue. We cannot conceptualize *nothing*, because all we know is the realm of *something*.

Astronomy tells us that the universe hasn't always existed. Instead, it popped into existence a finite time ago. While it's impossible for us to imagine, before there was something, there was nothing. Interestingly, this is the same story Jesus and the Book of Genesis tell.

Big bang cosmology and the laws of physics teach that the universe had an absolute beginning a fixed time ago. This conclusion rests on various factors, including the expanding nature of the universe, and the finite amount of energy within the universe. Reason affirms that a universe with no beginning is impossible (check out the toggle, *A Universe with No Beginning?*).

A Universe With no Beginning?

The Big Bang theory makes sense of the evidence. But it raises more questions than it answers. In affirming that *nothing* existed before there was *something*, we wonder where the something came from? And why did it suddenly appear out of nothing?

These questions are beyond the reach of science, which only observes and predicts causes and effects among existing physical things. Even so, in an attempt to explain the Big Bang in a way that preserves their assumption that something physical-like always existed, some physicists try to define the "nothing before the something" in theoretical terms.

A popular example was Carl Sagan's assertion

(following Edwin Hubble) that, before the Big Bang, the potential universe was contained in a "mathematical point with no dimensions at all... [possessing] extremely high density."[5]

Sounds scientific enough. But isn't he really just using *something* language to describe the *nothing* that preceded the universe? Isn't a mathematical point with no dimensions (size) just a theoretical place holder for nothing. To say this "point" of nothingness possesses infinite density is merely to say that there was an infinite amount of nothing before there was something. You be the judge as to whether that makes any sense. "Solutions" like this one fail to escape the logical problems with a beginning-less universe.

Bottom line: The physical sciences cannot adequately describe or explain anything earlier than the first moment of the existing universe (the first moment after the Big Bang). This leaves us with important and nagging questions, like, "Why is there something rather than nothing?" And, most puzzling of all, "How did something begin to exist out of nothing?"

---

5 Carl Sagan, Cosmos (New York: Ballantine Books, 1993) 201.

We have two basic ways we can answer this last question. The first approach is to dogmatically assert that something just *did* come from nothing, for no reason, without a cause. Of course, this assertion violates our rationality and all we know from science. This belief also requires an extraordinary amount of blind faith, though many whohold this view think they avoid the need for faith by suggesting the universe popped into existence by *chance*. The trouble is, chance does not and cannot *cause* anything. It only refers to possible ways that *existing* realities might interact with each other under certain circumstances.

To say there's a chance something might spontaneously pop into existence out of nothing is like saying there's a chance my non-existing twin brother will buy me an ice cream cone at the county fair. This is not even a possibility, because no such twin exists. Chance has no power to create or change reality.

The second way to answer the question, "How did something begin to exist out of nothing?" is to affirm with reason and intuition that something caused it to exist. Some try to find this cause within the pure *potential* of the universe. But, as we saw above and in the previous toggle, this theory makes no sense, because nothing (no potentialities) existed to cause anything. Moreover, it's a contradiction to say something caused itself to exist, because something must exist before it can act.[6]

The Universe was a Purposeful Choice

So the universe must have been caused by something outside itself, something separate and distinct from itself. But what was this cause? Was it impersonal, like a domino falling in a causal series? Or was it a personal agent who chose to create a universe that would not have come to be if this agent had not chosen to create it?

6 Stephen Hawking wrote, "Because there is a law such as gravity, the Universe can and will create itself from nothing..." Stephen Hawking and Leonard Mlodinow, The Grand Design (New Yord: Bantom Books, 2010) 180. Hawking must be using the term "nothing" in this statement to refer to something other than literal nothingness. Otherwise, his assertion is nonsensical. Luke Muehlhauser affirms,

> [Hawking's Book] does not even argue that the universe created itself from nothing, as nothing is usually conceived. Instead, Hawking argues that the universe will create itself from the pre-existing vacuum energy of "empty space," which, is not really empty...on Hawking's model, this quantum vacuum energy is only known to exist after time 0 (the "beginning" of the universe). So if you're looking for an explanation of how the universe could create itself from nothing, you won't find even an attempt at the answer in Hawking's book." Luke Muehlhauser, "Stephen Hawking – The Grand Design (review),"Common Sense Atheism, 12 July 2012 < http://commonsenseatheism.com/?p=12325>.

Check out the toggle, *The Universe Was a Purposeful Choice,* if you'd like to see why a personal cause to the universe makes the most sense. Of course, you don't need arguments to gain a belief in a Creator. You already know He is there and that you owe your existence to Him.

> For what can be known about God is plain to them [all people], because God has shown it to them [all people]. For his invisible attributes, namely, his eternal power and divine nature, have been clearly perceived, ever since the creation of the world, in the things that have been made. So they are without excuse."[7]

Our intuition tells us that we live in a personal universe, created by a personal, uncreated God (see the toggle, *Who Created God?* to see why God was not created). Science and reason affirm with our intuitions that a personal God is the beginning of the story we find ourselves in. This God created all things, including us, out of nothing, for His own purposes. The Bible affirms that the One who created us continues to hold us in exis-

Who Created God?

7 Romans 1:19-20

tence by His will,[8] so that, in every sense, we owe our existence to Him.

We'll talk more about this in chapter six. For now, what can we learn about our Creator by looking at the kind of universe He created?

To begin with, He must be immensely powerful to have created the cosmos out of nothing. In fact, He must be the source of *all* power, because, as we have seen, He is the backdrop of all existence.

The uncreated Creator of the universe must be completely self-sufficient, without need of anything or anyone outside Himself. And He must have tremendous intelligence to have designed and created the simple complexity of the universe. He must also be an artist who loves beauty, having sprinkled it throughout everything He made.

Aspects of our planet, such as how our intricate eco-systems work together to sustain the life He designed, reveal that our Creator is undeniably purposeful. No wonder He populated the earth with purposeful people who build purposeful relationships, chase dreams, and pursue the meaning they know is part of life.

---

8 Hebrews 1:3

God must also have a great sense of humor. Why else would He create smiling dolphins, sloths and blowfish, mischievous monkeys, crafty meerkats and people who love to laugh? Why did Jesus give some of his disciples funny nicknames that matched their personalities?[9] Because God has a sense of humor.

Our Creator must also be concerned with goodness, because basic morality is a self-evident reality in the universe. He made us to recognize the universe's moral fabric, pursue what is right and hold accountable those who do wrong.

But, someone might ask, if God is concerned with goodness, why is there so much evil in the world? This is a good question that isn't easy to answer; yet, answers are available. We will talk more about those answers later on our journey.

Finally, God must value relationships, because they are such a fundamental part of what He has made. Think about the personalities of animals and people, and how both form communities to experience life together. We'll see, as we move forward, that God is all about relationships, and that one of His highest priorities is for people to expe-

9 For example, see Luke 9:54, compared to Mark 3:17

rience relationship with Him.

He created us with the desire to know Him, which we see in our yearning to connect with perfect love, acceptance and purpose, and to worship something ultimate. Though we twist this longing into many forms, God clearly created us with the innate desire to encounter Him—which suggests He wants to be known by us, and leads us to expect that He has and will reveal Himself to us so we can build a relationship with Him. And, because our race is ancient, we should expect to find God's revelation of Himself in ancient human history, addressing mankind as a whole.

The idea of connecting with God hit a chord with my friends Johnny and Dave as we pursued the big story together. The fire within compelled them to connect with the God they knew was there. I invited them to begin looking for God's ancient revelation by focusing on the life and story of Jesus, not only because He is the most unique and revolutionary person who ever lived, but also because He claimed to reveal the God who created all things. Jesus also claimed He was the center of God's ancient revelation to man and backed up

His claims with words and actions that led many to believe He was, in fact, the climax of the story we find ourselves in, the one who fulfilled the ancient promises God gave to the very first human beings, and to Israel, His covenant people.

The life and words of Jesus, as recorded in the New Testament Gospels, put all the pieces together for me and taught my soul to sing. I invited my friends to investigate the person of Jesus and decide for themselves about the validity of the story He told of the God who was there before anything else—who created all things, including us, that we might know and enjoy Him forever. I invited them to consider the story of man's paradise in Eden with God, when things were as they ought to be on planet earth. I wanted them to hear the story of paradise lost through our rebellion against God, and God's promise to rescue us from our fall and renew all things through His Champion who has come—the *Messiah* or *Christ* of God.[10]

To really understand the story Jesus told, we must go back to the beginning with Him, to the

10 "Messiah" and "Christ are, respectively, the Hebrew and Greek renderings of the word that refers to God's anointed and promised Champion.

ancient story recorded in *Genesis,* the first book of the Bible. As we do, don't be surprised by how familiar this story sounds.

A Universe with No Beginning?

Mathematics makes a distinction between potential infinity and actual infinity. We must understand this distinction in order to talk meaningfully about the kind of universe we live in.

A potentially infinite set has an absolute starting point and grows (potentially) forever by adding new members to the set. An example of a potentially infinite set or series is: {1, 2, 3...}. A potential infinite in geometry would be represented by:

⟶

A potentially infinite row of dominos would have an absolute beginning (first domino) and be potentially infinite in length, because we could add dominos to the chain forever, as long as we didn't run out of dominos. Likewise, a potentially infinite universe would have an absolute starting point (first event) and continue (potentially) forever, depending on the amount of energy available for events within that universe.

An actually infinite series differs from a potentially infinite series, because an actually infinite series lacks a beginning point and an end point. An example of an actually infinite set or series is: {... 1, 2, 3...}. In geometry, an actual infinite looks like:

⟵⟶

It's impossible to point to an actually infinite series in the real world. But a bottomless pit or chain of dominos with no beginning (first domino) or end (last domino) would be examples of actually infinite series.

A potentially infinite series of events can be created by successively adding new events. But an actually infinite series exists all at once. It cannot be created through successive addition, because it already includes every possible member or event within it.

For the same reason that you cannot create an actually infinite series through successive addition, moving through an actually infinite series is impossible. For example, it's impossible to move from event one to event two in an actually infinite series, because there are an actually infinite number of events leading up to event one, and in-between event one and event two, just as there is an actually infinite number of events between each of the events in the series. Moving through an actually infinite series would be like trying to jump out of a bottomless pit—impossible by definition.

Consider another example. If there were such a thing as an actually infinite series of dominos, the series could never begin to fall, because there is no beginning point in the series, and between each domino there is an actually infinite number of dominos that must fall before any given domino could fall.

Let's apply this to the series of events that is our universe. While the universe can be a potentially infinite series of events moving outward from an absolute starting point, it cannot be an actually infinite series of events with no starting point. For, if the universe literally has no beginning (i.e., it consists of an actually infinite number of events leading to the present moment), then the present moment could never have arrived, because moving through an actually infinite series is impossible.

But our universe has a measurable history, and we have arrived at the present moment. We have moved and we are moving through the series of events that is our universe. Therefore, the universe cannot consist of an actually infinite (beginning-less) series of events.

Moreover, the universe cannot have existed forever because there is a finite amount of useable energy within it. Thus, if the universe were actually infinite in age, the usable energy in the universe would have burned out an infinite number of years ago. But humanity and the universe are still here. Therefore, the universe must not be actually infinite. Reason, together with science, affirms that our universe had an absolute beginning point, before which, it did not exist.

The Universe Was a Purposeful Choice

The cosmos were created by a personal, intelligent and purposeful being. Given the finiteness of the universe (see previous toggle note), this is the most logical conclusion and the best explanation of the data in front of us. We begin with logic and conclude with empirical evidence.

Whatever caused the universe, it either always existed (did not come to be) and therefore did not require a cause, or it came to be as the result of another cause. If the cause of the universe was itself caused, we could then ask what the cause of that cause was, and so forth.

We saw in the last toggle note that the universe had an absolute beginning, which implies at least one uncaused cause. This is the only way to avoid the impossibility of an actually infinite regression of causation.

While this uncaused (absolute) cause existed prior to the universe it caused, the existence of this absolute cause did not guarantee the universe would come to be, since that would imply that the cause of the universe was itself part of a necessary causal chain, and lead us back to the actually infinite regression we have already ruled out.

But if this absolute cause caused the universe when it might not have, then the absolute cause of the universe must have had the power to choose whether or not to cause it. In other words, the absolute cause of the universe was a person, a choosing agent.

Three types of empirical evidence bolster the conclusion that the universe was created by a personal, choosing agent:

1. The cosmic parameters of the universe
2. The peculiarity of our galaxy, solar system and planet; and

The complexity of life itself (I deal with this one in the next chapter)

Together, these three empirical realities lead me to conclude that the universe was not only created by a personal agent, but intentionally designed with (human) life in mind.

Consider our peculiar universe. Astronomers and physicists marvel at the precise balance of cosmic parameters that govern the cosmos. This is especially remarkable when you consider that the prerequisites for a universe to sustain life are exceedingly narrow. The probability of such a universe existing by chance is infinitesimally small.

And yet, these prerequisites exist in our universe, leading many to conclude that the cosmos are governed by what some scientists have dubbed the Anthropic Principle, because the universe appears to have been intentionally designed to sustain life, especially human life. These scientists draw this conclusion by extrapolating the smallest of changes in the foundational structures of the universe, only to find that even a tiny change in these components would cause the universe to implode on itself or become utterly hostile toward any form of life.

Astrophysicist, Hugh Ross, lists dozens of constants in the universe, any one of which, if altered even slightly, would make life impossible anywhere in the universe.* These constants include things like the number and kind of molecules, atoms, nucleons and electrons in the universe, all of which form in kind and number as a function of precise electromagnetic and nuclear forces.

In addition, he points out with other physicists, that the expansion rate of the universe had to be precisely what it is for life to form in our universe. If it had been slower, matter would have formed too densely. If faster, galaxies and stars would have never formed.

The same is true of the gravitational and electromagnetic forces in the universe—not to mention, the velocity of light, entropy rate, distance between stars, ratio between exotic and normal matter, etc. Similar life-necessary constraints govern galaxies, stars, solar systems, planets and moons.

Together with the life-necessary constraints on the universe as a whole, Ross argues, the likelihood of even one planet or moon capable of sustaining life accidentally is infinitesimally small.** If Ross and other astrophysicists are correct, the fact that life exists anywhere in the universe affirms our assertion that the universe is the result of a choosing agent, and again rebuts the claim that our universe popped into existence for no reason, without a cause. As we have seen in previous chapters, a personal creator is precisely what our experiences in this world lead us to expect.

*Hugh Ross, The Creator and the Cosmos, (Colorado Springs: Nav Press, 1993) 105-21.
** IBID, 123-135.

Who created God?

Only things that begin to exist require a cause. We saw in the last two toggles that the universe began to exist and, therefore, required a cause. But in order to avoid an actually infinite regression of causation, which, as we have seen, is impossible, there must be an ultimate cause, at least one uncaused cause behind our universe. If, as I argue throughout this book, God is this absolute cause of the universe, then, by definition, God did not begin to exist and, therefore, did not require a cause.

Interestingly, when God spoke to Moses in Exodus chapter 3, and Moses asked for God's name, God declared His name to be "I AM," which happens to be the Hebrew verb "to be." In other words, God says, "I am the (only) One who exists without beginning or end."

If you're like me, you find it difficult to imagine a truly beginning-less being. But this is precisely what our finite universe requires. It also points to the indescribable greatness of the One who made us. *Great is the LORD, and greatly to be praised, and his greatness is unsearchable.* (Psalm 145:3 ESV)

Chapter 5

Kiss of Life

Have you ever wondered who invented the kiss? Or how a little peck can make a grown man blush, woo a loved one or deepen romance? Why can't a head-butt or fist-bump accomplish the same thing?

And why are we so selective about who we kiss? If you're like me, you only press your lips against those you're closest to—because, for most of us, a kiss is a vulnerable expression of intimacy and affection.

Is it any wonder that human life began with a kiss? The Book of Genesis says so. "In the beginning, God created the heavens and earth."[11]

Who Wrote the Book of Genesis?

Then, after preparing the earth and atmosphere to support life, God created plants, fish and animals by speaking them into existence.

11 Genesis 1:1

But when God created mankind, He did something special. Instead of simply calling Adam (the first human being) into existence,

Did Adam and Eve Actually Exist?

> ...the LORD God formed the man of dust from the ground and **breathed into his nostrils the breath of life**, and the man became a living creature.[12]

Don't miss the divine romance in this, the very first scene in human history. After thoughtfully shaping Adam's body from the dust of the ground in the Garden of Eden, the God who has no beginning, need nor equal, humbly stoops to come face-to-face with Adam's lifeless form.

Pressing His face to Adam's, with an intimate "kiss," God lovingly breathes life into Adam's body so that Adam becomes a living person. The first thing Adam sees is the face of God. The first thing Adam knows is communion with God.

God's method was His message. He created us *in* and *for* a priority relationship with Him. This is why He made Adam and Eve separately, to ensure they understood that their most important relationship was with Him, not one another. And that,

---

12 Genesis 2:5-8

their *vertical* connection with God would form the basis and context for their *horizontal* relationship with each other. Let me explain. Having created Adam in a relationship with Him,

> "...the LORD God said, 'It is not good that the man should be alone; I will make him a helper fit for him.' So the LORD God caused a deep sleep to fall upon the man, and while he slept took one of his ribs and closed up its place with flesh. And the rib that the LORD God had taken from the man he made into a woman and brought her to the man. Then the man said, 'This at last is bone of my bones and flesh of my flesh; she shall be called Woman, because she was taken out of Man.' Therefore, a man shall leave his father and his mother and hold fast to his wife, and they shall become one flesh. And the man and his wife were both naked and were not ashamed."[13]

Did God Use Evolution to Make Us?

God created Adam and Eve to enjoy a deep and wonderful relationship with each other. But He created Eve from Adam's humanity only *after* He placed Adam in a soul-surrounding, self-defining relationship with Himself.

13 Genesis 2:18, 21-25

Indirectly, Eve's humanity came from the same divine kiss that brought Adam to life. And, like Adam, God created Eve for a priority relationship with Himself, not merely to be with Adam.

By God's design, our vertical relationship with Him defines who we are and gives context to our horizontal relationships with one another. This is because God created us "in His image" to know Him, and to reflect Him in the world through our relationships with one another.

Understanding what it means to bear God's image is crucial to understanding who we are, what it means to be human, and what our role is in this story we find ourselves in. Before creating mankind, God said:

> ...**Let us make man in our image** after our likeness... So God created man in his own image, in the image of God he created him; male and female he created them.[14]

To say God created us in His image means that we reflect God's nature in significant ways. God is creative—so are we. God is intelligent—we have the

14 Genesis 1:26-27

ability to reason. God is the center and source of morality—He created us to discern between good and evil. These are all ways we reflect God's image.

But, perhaps most significantly, we reflect God's relational image. God reveals this important aspect of His being when He says, "Let *Us* create man in *Our* image..." Why does God refer to Himself in the plural as He prepares to create mankind?

In the ancient world in which *Genesis* was written, a king might refer to himself as "We" and "Our," as a way to distinguish himself from non-royals. God may have used this kingly language when revealing the creation story to Moses, to make it clear that He (God) is the ultimate king.

Or perhaps God is speaking as you and I might speak when we are alone and in the midst of a creative project. We might think or say to ourselves, "Hmm, what shall we build today."

But most intriguing is a third way to understand why God refers to Himself in the plural: He may be introducing us to the plurality within His singular being.

God makes it increasingly clear as scripture unfolds that, though He is one being, He exists *in* and *as* a divine (triune) community of the Father, Son and Holy Spirit. Together, they is the one God. Bad grammar; good theology.

The plurality of persons within God's singular being is a mystery God reveals about Himself throughout the Bible. It will blow your mind if you try too hard to unpack it. But the triune, communal nature of God is a beautiful and necessary aspect of who He is. And, as I clarify in the toggle, *What is the Trinity*, it's at the core of God's intensely relational nature.

What is the Trinity?

Interestingly, God revealed His relational, communal nature right before He declared that mankind would reflect His image. This suggests that one of the most important ways we reflect God's image is through *our* relational, communal nature, revealed in our deep longing for relationship with God and others.

As we have seen, God created us for a priority, self-defining relationship with Him that shapes and compels meaningful relationships with each other. Putting it all together, the God who is communal by nature created us in and for community, first with Himself and then with one another.

Eden was paradise for Adam and Eve, not merely because it was a beautiful place, but primarily because, in the garden, they enjoyed unbroken fellowship with the God whose image they bore. Their relationship with Him anchored their identity as human beings and set them free to love and serve one another, without fear of rejection or failure.

They knew who they were vertically (toward God), and therefore, horizontally (toward each other). They were naked (completely vulnerable), yet unashamed (without insecurity). Together, God called them to enjoy a perfect relationship with the rest of creation by obeying His command to rule over and cultivate the earth.[15]

In Eden, Adam and Eve tasted the essence of life. They experienced the beauty, fullness, connection and joy we long to know. The ancient Hebrews called this, *shalom*, a state of perfect peace with God that brings peace within ourselves, with one another, and with the rest of creation. To top it off, God called Adam and Eve to a life-long mission of great importance. Specifically, God called them to

15 Genesis 2:15

"be fruitful and multiply and fill the earth."[16]

Contrary to popular belief, God wasn't just calling this naked couple to make babies. Yes, this was part of their purpose. But the heart of their mission was to fill the earth with others like them—people who would join them in enjoying a self-defining, vertical relationship with God that would, in turn, shape their horizontal relationships with one another and the world.

Ultimately, the command to be fruitful and multiply was a call to fill the earth with God's glory, which is mankind's greatest privilege and deepest joy. Why? Because, in the beginning, *God!*

Everything comes *from* Him, exists *for* Him and points to Him. Nothing exists apart from God. All meaning and purpose begin and end with Him. God created the heavens and the earth to fill them with His glory. He created us in His image to know and enjoy Him forever, by reflecting His image in the world.

God is the light of life. As the moon has no light of its own, but only reflects the light of the sun, we have no light of our own, but exist to reflect

16 Genesis 1:28

the light of God's glory. From the beginning, God planned to fill the earth with His glory, by filling it with worshipers, created beings who would bask in His glory and reflect His beauty on the earth.

In this sense, the Garden of Eden was God's temple. By calling Adam and Eve to fill the earth with worshipers, He was calling them to expand the temple of Eden until it covered the whole earth. Later in history, God called His covenant people (Israel) to build a temple for Him. He commanded them to decorate it with scenes from nature, pointing back to the first temple in Eden (the way things were). The ornamentation also pointed forward to the day when God would fulfill His original plan to fill the earth with His glory. More on that later. For now, understand that in Eden, Adam and Eve enjoyed beauty, love, purpose and perfection in Him. They sang the song we were all meant to sing together, in the presence of the One who made us for Himself and taught us the ancient melody of shalom.

In the next chapter, we'll see what went wrong in Eden and why we're no longer living in paradise. For now, remember that in our search for the story we find ourselves in, the best story wins.

That is, the story behind it all will account for the details of life as it *is*, and *ought* to be.

Let's take a moment to evaluate how the ancient story from Genesis satisfies our deepest intuitions about who we are and what it means to be us.

Unlike the "physical-stuff only" stories that make no room for souls or selves, the Genesis story accounts for both. Specifically, God created us as physical and spiritual persons who interact in the spiritual and physical realms (with God, and in His creation).

The Eastern stories (Hinduism and Buddhism) insist we live in an impersonal universe, void of actual persons. The Genesis story affirms our intuition that we were created as personal beings, by a personal God, for a relationship with Him and one another.

The "physical-stuff only" story claims we are just products of time plus chance, living in an impersonal, random universe. But if that's true, where do we get the intrinsic value we know we possess as human beings? The Genesis story anchors our value in our reflection of God's image.

And what about good and evil? We saw in Chapter Three that morality is grounded in an absolute standard, which neither the "physical-stuff only" nor Eastern stories can provide. But the Genesis story points to God, our creator, as the basis for morality, satisfying our intuition that morality is inherently personal, and most at home in a personal universe created by a personal God.

Finally, neither the "physical-stuff only" nor Eastern stories provide us with the kind of purpose and meaning we long for. But Genesis affirms that each of us is part of a beautiful love story, in which we were created for a face-to-face relationship with the God of the universe. This God calls us to fill the earth with His perfection and glory, as we enjoy vertical relationships with Him that shape our horizontal relationships with one another. Genesis calls us to pursue, enjoy and multiply life on earth as it was meant to be.

And so, before we move on, I invite you to experience the déjà vu of a place called Eden, and a life called shalom. Can you hear the echo of the song our ancient parents sang?

Listen for the melody again. Follow it if you dare—back to Eden.

Who wrote the Book of Genesis?

Genesis is one of the first five books of the Bible known as the Pentateuch. The Pentateuch claims a man named Moses for its author. See, for example, Exodus 17:14 and Deuteronomy 31:9. Long before the time of Jesus, Jews were already dividing the Jewish scriptures (Old Testament) into the Books of Moses, the Prophets and the Psalms.

Jesus affirmed this order, including the authorship of the Pentateuch by Moses. For example, He says in Luke 24:44, "I told you that everything written about me by Moses and the prophets and in the Psalms must all come true."

Moses wrote the Book of Genesis, together with the rest of the Pentateuch, as he prepared Israel to enter the promised land of Palestine around 1400 B.C. He wrote these words to remind the Jewish nation that they were God's people, because, for many generations, they'd been slaves in Egypt.

Orthodox Jews and Christians believe that God is the ultimate author of scripture, including the Pentateuch. More specifically, God has revealed Himself and His plans to mankind by speaking to and through people called prophets, who accurately recorded God's words in sacred scripture.

Several factors bolster this claim, including the origin of the scriptures themselves. For example, the Jewish (Old) Testament was written over a one thousand-year period, by dozens of people from many walks of life, including kings, peasants, shepherds, philosophers and farmers.

These writers represented a great breadth of life experience, in the vast geography of Africa and Asia. Some were rich, others poor. Some were free, others oppressed. But whatever their differences, these authors were united in the story they told.

The consistency with which they told and expanded the story of God's covenant people, while progressively clarifying the meaning and destiny of God's redemptive program, is astounding—especially when one considers the vast amount of time and distance that separated them. Yet, each in his own time and place declared, "Thus says the Lord...," without ever contradicting one another. No wonder the Jewish scribes were so meticulous in preserving the integrity and content of the text they received.

In addition to the divine inspiration and protection of the sacred narrative, fulfilled prophecy is further evidence of divine providence over the Jewish scriptures. Instances of this phenomenon are abundant. For example, Ezekiel's detailed prophecy against Tyre (Ezekiel 26-27) was fulfilled in a way that can still be verified in detail today. In the same way, the pinpoint accuracy of the Prophet Daniel's predictions regarding the kingdoms that would rule on the earth after the Babylonians, leading up to the time of Christ, is uncanny.

Perhaps most impressive are the copious and detailed prophecies about the Messiah's identity, birthplace, life, death and resurrection that were precisely fulfilled in the historical person of Jesus.

Finally, many point to the lives transformed by the self-authenticating power of God's Word as evidence to God's authorship of the scriptures through human beings like Moses.

Did Adam and Eve Actually Exist?

What are we to do with Adam and Eve? Are they just poetic ideas? Fables? Metaphors? Or were they actual people like you and me? Did the human race begin, as the Book of Genesis insists, near the Tigris and Euphrates rivers in Africa, with one man and one woman in relationship with God and one another? Several streams of evidence support the assertion that Adam and Eve were historical figures in space-time history.

First, belief in a literal Adam and Eve was part of the Jewish tradition, in which Jesus identified Himself. Thus, in Luke 3:38, Luke extends the genealogy of Jesus all the way back to Adam (obviously leaving gaps but hitting key figures along the way, as was the custom in this period). Furthermore, while Jesus does not refer to Adam or Eve by name, he refers to them indirectly by quoting Moses' words about them in Genesis 1-2.

Significantly, He does this to ground His teaching about marriage and divorce in the creation design of God:

"But from the beginning of creation, 'God

made them male and female.' 'Therefore a man shall leave his father and mother and hold fast to his wife, and the two shall become one flesh..." (Mark 10:6-7).

Jesus' careful quotation of Genesis confirms that he accepted the creation account of Genesis 1-2. In this context of an absolute beginning, he affirms that God created man—male and female. Given that most Jews would have accepted the historical reality of Adam and Eve, Jesus' simple, unqualified mention of their beginning and relationship should be understood as an affirmation of their historicity.

Anthropology and biochemistry provide a second stream of evidence. Specifically, tracing mitochondrial DNA origins, which are passed exclusively from a mother to her offspring, scientists have traced the origin of man to a single female ancestor in sub-Saharan Africa, not far from where Biblical scholars believe the Garden of Eden was located. Scientists have ironically referred to this woman as the mother of humanity or "Eve."

Many scientists agree that humanity began with a single female and, presumably, a single male.

They differ on what happened before this point, but it is fascinating that they trace our race back to a single woman in ancient Africa. If, as I have suggested, life is impossible apart from creation, then we should expect to find an Adam and an Eve.

Some resist the idea that Adam and Eve were the absolute beginning of humanity, due to their commitments to various theories of evolution. They even point to supposed hominid precursors that appeared before mankind. But their repeated adjustments of time frames and assumptions surrounding these presumed precursors betray the fact that they are far from certain about what really happened, and what or who these so-called precursors really were.

This is not to suggest that creationists don't have challenges of their own when it comes to dates, fossils and so forth. We must humbly admit there are details about our origins we do not, and perhaps cannot, know with certainty. But many factors lead me to embrace the Genesis narrative as history: (1) the impossibility of the universe popping into existence for no reason, without a cause, (2) the virtual impossibility of abiogenesis (life popping out of non-life), (3) the lack of clear transitional forms in the fossil record to support Darwinian macro-evolution (see the next toggle for a defense of these last two assertions), (4) the inability of physicalistic theories to explain the most important things in life, and (5) the world we live in leads us to the deep expectation of an ancient revelation from God to reveal Himself to us; and, for reasons I have mentioned and will expand on in future chapters, the best candidate for this revelation is the Bible. From all these things, I conclude that the Genesis story is at least as good as its closest competitors, and, I believe, distinguishes itself as the beginning of the story we find ourselves in.

Did God Use Evolution to Make Us?

The term, *evolution*, generally refers to a family of theories that assume life on earth originated from random, non-rational, purely physical processes. Long ago, we are told, a single-cell organism formed accidentally through the random interaction of chemicals and energy in an ancient primordial soup. This pool of chemicals, like the chemicals themselves, had formed purely by chance. Ultimately, the theory continues, accidental mutations (changes) within this first accidental organism eventually produced other, increasingly complex and varied organisms, which led to all the species on earth.

Most evolutionists deny that an intelligent designer was required for life to form. Instead, they begin with a philosophical (religious?) commitment to physicalism, the belief that only physical stuff exists. This is why they insist that life is solely the product of chemistry, physics and random (physical) mutations. Of course, they cannot justify their belief that only physical stuff exists by using the physical sciences. Their most foundational belief is ultimately an article of faith, upon which their physicalistic theories stand. This is ironic at best, self-refuting at worst.

Not only that, but if physicalism is true, and our minds are the product of non-rational, random forces, one wonders how (physicalist) scientists can claim to "know" anything, since, to be consistent, their mental processes and conclusions would be nothing more than the product of non-rational, random causes.

Be that as it may, and setting aside the question of where the original pool of chemicals came from, macro-evolutionary theory is riddled with problems. To understand why, we need to understand the roots of these theories. Though others postulated the possibility of evolution prior to Charles Darwin, with the writing of The Origin of the Species in 1859, Darwin captured the world's imagination with a palpable, testable theory of how life formed on earth.

To his credit, Darwin observed what has become the well-documented process of micro-evolution. This process is the ability of members within a given species to adapt to their environment over time, a remarkable capacity to be sure, affirming the creative complexity built into their DNA. But, while his observations were sound, Darwin over-reached with his inductive conclusion that macro-evolution (species gradually mutating into new and distinct species) took place. This conclusion was unwarranted by what he observed. More importantly, it has been refuted by the very standard he established for himself.

Darwin stated that his theory would stand or fall on what the fossil record would reveal in the decades after he offered his theory. The proof, Darwin understood, would be in the paleontology (fossil discovery and classification). And what has paleontology revealed? The exact opposite of what Darwin postulated. To vindicate Darwinism, the fossil record would have had to reveal an abundance of clear examples of progressive transition between species. In other words, if Darwin was correct, there should be large numbers of intermediary forms between species.

But these intermediary forms are conspicuously absent from the fossil record. The strata are replete with fully formed, distinct species, but leave no clear evidence of gradual, mutational changes between species. Of course, those who begin with the assumption that Darwin was correct insist that mere similarities or shared characteristics between species affirm his theory.

However, these presumptive lenses obscure the fact that not a single, non-controversial, intermediary form exists in the fossil record. If Darwin's theory was correct, such examples would be abundant, varied and obvious to all. Instead, the record reveals fully formed "kinds" or species that appear, go extinct or continue to the present day.

The most notable example of this phenomenon is known as the Cambrian Explosion. It's called an explosion because animals representing every body type appear "suddenly" in the Cambrian strata. There are different views on how to date this strata. Geologists committed to a strict, gradualist view of geology date this period to five-hundred million years ago. Others, like those inclined toward catastrophic geological explanations, believe this strata is much younger.

Geologists also debate if and how various geological strata are isolated from, and blend into one another. But, regardless of their presuppositions, prior to the appearance of an abundance of fully formed species in the Cambrian layer, the strata reveal only a small handful of the most basic forms of life. After the Cambrian period, there is a consistent, gradual decrease in animal body types, leading up to the present day.

The Cambrian Explosion points to the exact opposite of what Darwin theorized. Instead of small gradations that produced new species from old ones, we find a variety of fully formed species existing all at once, alongside each other. The fossil record simply does not substantiate Darwin's macro-evolutionary claim.

A second problem with physicalistic, macro-evolution takes us back to the so-called primordial soup of chemicals that spontaneously and accidentally produced a living creature that became the ancestor of all life on earth. This belief begins with the incredible assumption that just the right chemicals happened to form in just the right place at just the right time and in just the right quantity, on an earth and in a universe that popped into existence, for no reason, without a cause.

Add to these remarkable leaps of faith the belief that a spark of energy in just the right measure, at precisely the right moment, struck this pool of chemicals in just the right spot to cause a reaction that produced a living cell. This theoretical process is known as abiogenesis (life from non-life). Of course, this is all conjecture, because no known mechanism or system exists to make abiogenesis occur.

Even after one-hundred fifty years of (intelligent) research, plus billions of dollars invested in our brightest minds and best technologies, humans have been unable to produce from scratch even the most basic machinery of a living cell (e.g., a protein) in the laboratory. But the formation of even the simplest cell requires that all its many components exist all at once, in precisely the same place, and at the same time.

The cell ingredients must come together and bond to one another, while simultaneously being surrounded by a cell membrane that protects the fragile unit of complex parts. How ironic that, even when we apply our intelligence, controlled environments and technology, we cannot even begin to do what some suggest a random, non-rational process did!

It seems to me that the more intelligence, resources and technology required to build even the most basic components of a cell from scratch (something we have not yet done), the less likely it is that an entire cell could have spontaneously been formed by non-intelligent, random forces. No wonder many scientists defend various forms of theistic evolution or intelligent design, in which God was involved in the evolutionary process. They understand that the process of evolution, if it really happened, could not be driven solely by random, non-rational forces.

Finally, the story of non-rational, physicalistic evolution fails because it cannot account for the most important realities of life. For example, if everything really is the product of time plus chance and physical stuff, then good and evil, beauty and souls are impossible. They are nothing more than illusions. In the same way, love, purpose and relationships would be meaningless games we play to pretend we are more than just random, purposeless bundles of chemicals.

But we know that we are more than purposeless bundles of chemicals, and that life is bigger than the unlikely story of abject, random meaninglessness. Interestingly, the Book of Genesis affirms what our intuitions suspect is true about life's origins. Genesis leaves some questions unanswered, and good people disagree on time-frames and how all the pieces fit together. But given the ridiculousness of something coming from nothing, for no reason, without a cause, compounded by the seeming impossibility of abiogenesis, the lack of support in the fossil record, and the inability of this story to account for the most important things in life, physicalistic evolution is a poor candidate for the big story that explains it all.

In this light, the story of Genesis becomes highly plausible, reminding us that God is the Creator of all life, and that He created fixed species according to His design. We are not random bundles of stuff, but purposeful, physical and spiritual beings made to experience beauty, encounter love and taste the richness of life in a relationship with the God who made us for this purpose.

What is the Trinity?

Though the word "trinity" is not found in the Bible, it was used in the early Church to describe the nature of God as recorded in the Bible, which teaches there is only one living and true God (Dt. 6:4; Is. 45:5-7; 1 Cor. 8:4). This one God is spirit by nature (John 4:24) and perfect in all His attributes. God is one in essence, eternally existing in three Persons—Father, Son, and Holy Spirit (Matt 28:19; 2 Cor. 13:14), who are co-eternal in nature, being, power and glory, identical in attributes and perfections, and equally deserving of worship and obedience.

The Biblical doctrine of the Trinity denies tri-theism (three gods) and modalism (one God appearing in different forms at different times). Tri-theism misunderstands the distinction between the three members of the divine essence or Godhead. Modalism misunderstands the unity within the Godhead.

The Father, Son and Holy Spirit share the unique essence of the one and only God. Each is a distinct instance of the single, divine essence. Together, they exist in eternal, essential relationship with one another, so that, together, they "is" the one and only God.

Why is God a Trinity? At one level, it's absurd for us to ask why God is the way He is, for He is God and we are not. But it is sometimes easier to encounter and walk with Him when we understand a few "whys" along the way. The fact that God is triune makes perfect sense when you consider that:

(1) There is only one God.

(2) God is unchanging, self-sufficient and eternally expressing all His perfect attributes.

(3) One of God's attributes is love.

(4) Love is necessarily other-focused.

Since love is one of God's attributes that has been expressed perfectly for eternity, and love is, by definition, others-focused, it follows that God has been loving another (or others) for eternity. This implies that an object of His love has been in existence for eternity. But only God is eternal. So the object(s) of God's love must exist within His eternal being.

The Trinity allows for a plurality of persons within the singular being of God, which, in turn, allows God to be loving, self-sufficient and eternal all at once. He is the absolute, eternal, divine community, and He invites us to enjoy communion with Him.

Chapter 6

Black Holes and the Law of Gravity

My brother Pat was the master. Our oldest brother, Tim, and I (the youngest), knew we could count on Pat to make our summers interesting. He had a gift. To this day, I'm not sure how he convinced that game warden to give adolescent boys a box of M-80 explosives, each of which could blow all the fingers off a hand in a single blast. But he did.

"We need some M-80s," Pat told the warden, "to keep those darn pheasants out of our corn." Of course, we didn't have any corn and we didn't care about pheasants. But we loved free explosives and used them to blow up pretty much anything we could get our hands on.

We also discovered how to launch tennis balls into orbit using an irrigation pipe as a canon. And, through creative experimentation, we learned the M-80s were water proof. We could "fish" with them!

My most memorable moment with the M-80s came at a 4-H camp I attended one summer with my brothers in the Donnelly forest. After smuggling our explosive's into camp, we searched for ways to put them to use.

Naturally, Pat came up with a brilliant idea. With six of us boys gathered around him, he placed an M-80 into the pouch of his wrist-rocket sling shot. "Go ahead," he said, aiming the explosive straight up. "Light it." One of us lit the fuse.

Pat watched it burn for a second or two and then shot it high into the forest air. Wide-eyed, we all followed it's flight upward, waiting with adrenalized anticipation for the air-burst to come.

But the fuse seemed to be burning much more slowly than the M-80 was now descending. "Hey," someone said. "It's coming down."

Panic set in. "It's coming DOWN. LOOK OUT, IT'S COMING DOWN!"

Bumping into each other like circus clowns, we scrambled to avoid the pending explosion. The M-80 detonated at about eye level and the blast reverberated through the forest. Amazingly, nobody lost an eye or an ear drum. Even so, in a rare display of wisdom, we decided not to try it again.

Through that memorable experience, we learned (among other things) that gravity waits for no one. What goes up must come down. Gravity ensures the return trip. Though we usually take gravity for granted, it has a way of reminding us of its presence through "4-H camp" moments.

When we think about it, we realize what a crucial role gravity plays in our everyday lives. We need just the right amount to experience life as we know it. Too little gravity, and we'd all float away. Too much gravity would crush us.

Nowhere is this more obvious than with the gravity-gone-wild power of a black hole, which forms when a huge star explodes at the end of its life, leaving a dense mass of neutrons called a neutron star. No longer balanced by the outward-thrusting energy it had as a living star, the gravity caused by the core's density causes the star to implode upon itself, dragging all nearby matter, energy, light and sound into its irreversible vortex. This becomes what scientists call a black hole, because it's no longer pushing energy and light outward; instead, it's imploding inward, and nothing can escape its crushing darkness.

The imploding force of a black hole is a good analogy for what happened next in Eden, when the lights went out in paradise, as our first parents plunged themselves and us under the crushing darkness of what the Bible calls "sin."

Understanding what we lost with them is the first step to returning to the way we were and learning to sing again.

After creating Adam in Eden,

> "The LORD God commanded the man, 'You are free to eat from any tree in the garden; but you must not eat from the tree of the knowledge of good and evil, for when you eat of it you will surely die.'"[17]

Immediately after creating Adam, God created Eve, so that together, they would reflect God's image in the paradise of Eden through their enduring obedience to Him. The tree of "the knowledge of good and evil" became the symbol of this obe-

17 Genesis 2:16-17

dience. "If you obey me," God said, "you will stay connected to me and live. If you rebel and thereby disconnect from me, you will die. You will corrupt and destroy yourselves and forfeit shalom—life as it was meant to be."

The choice was plain. Bliss in submission to God, disaster apart from Him. But why were these the only choices? Why no middle ground? Because of the law of gravity.

As physical gravity rules the physical universe, spiritual gravity governs the spiritual realm. For example, if a space-walking astronaut cuts the line that tethers him to his spaceship, the gravity of the densest nearby object will drag him away from his ship (source of life) and isolate him to death as he drifts into oblivion.

In the same way, God created us to be tethered to Him. He is the source, center and meaning of all things. He is our anchor, the force that keeps us from being dragged into spiritual isolation and oblivion.

Because we are created in God's image, *we* are the densest nearby object when we push away from Him.

Therefore, when we cut the tether between us and God by shifting our focus from Him to ourselves, our self-centered rebellion causes us to implode into ourselves, and into the spiritual darkness.

Again we may ask, why is the result of our rebellion against God so drastic? We get a hint of the answer from the name of the forbidden tree—"the tree of the knowledge of good and evil."

Now, why would God forbid man to eat from a tree that would bring him knowledge? Isn't knowledge a good thing? Apparently not always, because man could only *know* evil by *doing* evil, by rebelling against the source and center of life.

Adam and Eve enjoyed paradise in Eden because all they knew (experienced) was goodness. While they knew *about* evil (the possibility of rebelling against God), they hadn't yet participated *in* evil, so as to know it intimately.

But God was fully acquainted with both good and non-good (evil). For God, this knowledge was not a problem, because He is *necessarily* good. He cannot do anything but perfect good, even when He interacts with evil.

Man is not like God in this sense. Though we were created in God's moral image, unlike God, we are not *necessarily* good, which means we are vulnerable to the polluting effects of evil. God knew that once we participated in evil, even for a moment, it would warp, twist and ultimately destroy us. Rebelling against God in order to know evil would tear Adam and Eve away from Him and expose them to the destruction that evil always brings by opposing, reversing and corrupting what is good.

God graciously warned Adam and Eve to avoid their own demise by fixing their gaze on Him. Unfortunately, our first parents ignored this warning and surrendered themselves to evil, by following the evil impostor who had crashed their party:

> Now the serpent was more crafty than any of the wild animals the LORD God had made. He said to the woman, "Did God really say, 'You must not eat from any tree in the garden'?"

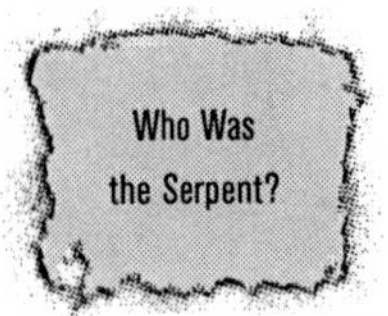

> The woman said to the serpent, "We may eat fruit from the trees in the garden, but God did say, 'You must not eat fruit from the tree that is in the middle of the garden, and you must not touch it, or you will die.'"

> "You will not surely die," the serpent said to the woman. **"For God knows that when you eat of it your eyes will be opened, and you will be like God, knowing good and evil."**[18]

"God is holding out on you," insists the lying serpent. "Though He's given you many good things, He's hoarding the best for Himself. God is keeping you from achieving your full potential, from being all you can be. But don't worry. I can help you get everything you deserve. I can help you be like God! Just take a bite."

Adam and Eve bought the lie.

> When the woman saw that the fruit of the tree was good for food and pleasing to the eye, **and also desirable for gaining wisdom**, she took some and ate it. She also gave some to her husband, who was with her, and he ate it.[19]

Was God Tempting
Adam and Eve
with the Tree?

God created us with the power to shape our destiny. This is a freedom we cherish and often defend as an inalienable right. This human capacity reflects the image of God in us. As such, it's a beautiful

18 Genesis 3:1-5

19 Genesis 3:6

thing when used rightly. But as Adam and Eve discovered, our capacity for self-determination brings deep ugliness when we use it to rebel against Him. No wonder, after rebelling against God,

> ...the eyes of both of them were opened, and **they realized they were naked**; so they sewed fig leaves together and made coverings for themselves. Then the man and his wife heard the sound of the LORD God as he was walking in the garden in the cool of the day, and they **hid from the LORD God** among the trees of the garden.
>
> But the LORD God called to the man, "Where are you?" He answered, "I heard you in the garden, and **I was afraid because I was naked; so I hid myself.**"[20]

Before their rebellion, Adam and Eve enjoyed paradise in Eden because their lives were *upward* focused—God-focused. Like the light of a star shining brightly in the heavens, their lives shone brightly in the presence of God and His creation.

But then their gaze shifted. Turning away from God, they began to worship themselves. But we

20 Genesis 3:7-10

weren't made to worship ourselves. Such weight is too great for our souls to bear. So spiritual gravity crushed Adam and Eve under the density of their self-worship.

God was no longer their vision. He no longer held their gaze and, therefore, He no longer held them. Spiritual gravity dragged them downward into a bottomless pit of darkness and isolation apart from God. No longer shining upward and outward, they were turned inside-out and upside-down.

No longer tethered to the God whose image they bore, they imploded under the weight of their self-focused rebellion. Disconnected from the source of life, they lost their individual sense of identity, which destroyed their ability to love, trust and serve one another without fear. Pushing away from God, they drifted away from one another.

Isolated, lonely and obsessed with themselves, they forfeited all they had known in Eden. Broken, twisted and crushed by the darkness, they became what they were never meant to be.

But even as they hid themselves from God, He graciously pursued them.

> And he said, "Who told you that you were naked? Have you eaten from the tree that I commanded you not to eat from?"[21]

No longer sure of themselves or one another, Adam and Eve were afraid to own up to what they had done.

> The man said, "The woman *you* put here with me—*she* gave me some fruit from the tree, and I ate it." Then the LORD God said to the woman, "What is this you have done?" The woman said, "The serpent deceived me, and I ate."[22]

Like lovers in crime who panic under interrogation and begin pointing their fingers at one another, Adam and Eve desperately search for somewhere to place their guilt and shame. Eve blames the serpent, but only after Adam turns against her.

Amazingly, Adam blames God for "the woman you (God) put here."[23] His words must have stung Eve's heart as much as they revealed the isolation Adam now felt from both God and Eve. And their

---

21 Genesis 3:11

22 Genesis 3:12-13

23 Genesis 3:12

pain would only go deeper.

> To the woman he said, "I will greatly increase your pains in childbearing; with pain you will give birth to children. Your desire will be for your husband, and he will rule over you."[24]

Remember, Eve was created for a loving relationship with Adam. Together, they were to fill the earth with a giant family. Partnering with Adam and anticipating her family relationships were at the heart of Eve's joy in paradise.

But now, as her vertical relationship with God was broken, her horizontal relationships would be too. Bearing children, though still a joy, would involve greatly increased pain, struggle and risk.

More significantly, the perfect love and partnership that once came naturally to this first marriage would be replaced by an ongoing struggle for harmony. Selfishness and the desire for control would forever tempt husbands and wives to fight with, rather than partner with, each other. But not even this was the end of their troubles.

---

24 Genesis 3:16

> To Adam he said, "Because you listened to your wife and ate from the tree about which I commanded you, You must not eat of it. **Cursed is the ground** because of you; through painful toil you will eat of it all the days of your life. It will produce thorns and thistles for you, and you will eat the plants of the field. By the sweat of your brow you will eat your food **until you return to the ground**, since from it you were taken; for dust you are and **to dust you will return**."[25]

God had placed Adam in the garden and called him to cultivate the earth and enjoy its fruits. Eve joined him in this task. But as the head of his race and family, working the ground and providing for his clan was Adam's calling.

Now, because of his rebellion against God, the ground was cursed along with him who was meant to cultivate it. No longer would the earth yield abundant fruit with minimal effort as it did in Eden. His work would become painful and difficult. Instead of working in harmony with the creation in Eden, Adam would wrestle with the earth to receive its spoils.

25 Genesis 3:17-19

The curse of their sin not only alienated Adam and Eve from God, themselves, and one another, but from the creation itself. And worst of all, man would no longer live forever as he was created to live. Instead, God declared to Adam, "to dust you will return."

Nothing feels quite as unnatural and unsettling as death. Sure, we've gotten used to it as a fact of life. But this new normal wasn't part of God's original design for us. This is why we dread the word "cancer," fight our mortality and mourn the loss of loved ones so deeply.

Death would never have come, had Adam and Eve stayed connected to the source of life. Because of their rebellion against Him, their spiritual death made physical death a way of life. Shalom was lost as Adam and Eve plunged themselves under the corrupting curse of sin. And because the entire human race was there in Adam at the fall, we all reap the consequences of the day the lights went out and the music died—the day we abandoned Eden and lost our way.

We all feel the weight of this fall, especially the evil unleashed within us that increasingly perverts our humanity. Though we've become experts at denying and suppressing this truth, in quiet moments of honest reflection, no amount of self-talk or positive spin can remove our profound sense that something is wrong, that we are fundamentally broken. And this brokenness shows up in every aspect of our lives.

Our Relationships

Imploding into ourselves and away from the One who defines us, we fight to salvage our identity through relationships with others, hoping someone's love will tell us who we are. This desperation often leads to unhealthy, over-dependent connections. And when people fail to make us whole, as they always do, our sense of self fails with them, leading to new feelings of rejection, isolation and loneliness.

We were made to find our identity in the One whose image we bear. Our vertical relationship with God is the only thing that can rightly shape our sense of self and allow us to share full and healthy relationships with others. When we find our identity in Him, instead of fear, insecurity and impossible expectations, we become healthy human beings who cultivate loving, committed and lasting relationships with others.

Our Endeavors

Disconnected from the One who gives us purpose, we strive for identity and meaning by filling our lives with activity and accomplishments. But no matter how many achievements we score, we always feel the need for more. No accomplishment can bring us the sense of purpose we find in communion with Him. This is because we were made to *do* what flows *from* our relationship with God. True satisfaction comes only when we understand that who we are is not defined by what we do, but by our union with the source of all life.

Our Addictions

Separated from the source of life, we are broken and insecure, longing for wholeness and certainty. Until we find true peace in Him, we look to people, things or experiences to make us feel significant, loved and whole. To numb our wounded souls, we overeat, over shop, over drink, or turn to gaming, TV or drugs. To relieve our anxiety, we addict ourselves to pornography, social networking or sitcoms. To find our identity, we binge and purge, cut, lose ourselves in our work, or obsess over hobbies and toys.

Our addictions help us escape our pain for a time, but life piles up while we're escaping, and the downward spiral continues, unless and until we return to shalom with Him.

Our Character

Adam and Eve rebelled against God because they wanted to be the center of their world. When we rebel against God, we do the same. The problem is, we are *not* God, and, therefore, we are not capable of defining or sustaining what is right and good in and of ourselves. For this reason, our rebellion against God twists and contorts our souls toward evil (non-good).

This evil in our souls leads to our "every-man-for-himself," "I deserve to be worshiped" world. Even our desire for relationships with others is often driven by our selfishness, riddling our families with dysfunction.

Every people group and community faces physical, emotional and sexual abuse. We oppress and exploit one another when given the opportunity. Clergy molest children. Husbands abuse wives. Children despise parents. Genocide rapes our planet, and selfishness drives rampant poverty.

We find new reasons to hate each other every day, and feel entitled to hoard that which billions in our world lack to survive. Even our sense of "doing good" has been corrupted by the fall. We no longer do good simply because it is right, but because it makes us feel satisfied with ourselves.

"Now hold on a minute," someone says. "I'm not perfect, but I'm not as bad as (*insert well known bad guy here*)." We can always find someone worse than us in some aspect of life. Yet, if we're honest, we all feel the sting of Jesus' words as He levels the playing field and reminds us that hate is the sin of murder. Lust is the sin of adultery. And, ultimately, the motivations of our hearts are what define and shape our character.[26]

The disturbing reality is that you and I possess the same capacity for sin expressed by the most

26 See Matthew 5-7

evil people we know. Even as we condemn the rapist, murderer, Nazi or corrupt politician, deep down, we know we're just like them. And if people could see the thoughts that go through our minds each day, they would know it, too.

Admitting the darkness within us can be overwhelming. It requires courage. The story Jesus told (beginning in Genesis) is filled with justice, forgiveness, hope and renewal. But before we get to these beautiful aspects of the story, we must take an honest look in the mirror and acknowledge who we really are—the fallen children of Adam and Eve. Sinners by nature *and* by choice, disconnected from the source of life, we no longer shine as we once did.

We may know how to survive, but we've forgotten how to thrive. Like the echo of a distant past, we remember who we were and the melody that burned brightly within. But our hearts have grown cold, and we've forgotten the tune. Weary, broken, wrestling in the dark, we long for the way we were. Our deepest desire is to find our way back to Eden, to defy the law of gravity and become human again.

Who Was the Serpent?

In Genesis 3, the serpent is none other than the devil himself—Satan, the adversary of God and His people. Little is revealed in the Bible about the origin and corruption of the devil, but a few points are clear. In Isaiah 14, God rebukes a rebellious king, using terms that point beyond this king's earthly rule to Lucifer, a mighty fallen angel. God refers to this angel as "day star," or "morning star" and "son of the dawn."

Through the Prophet Ezekiel, God says of this angel:

> You were the signet of perfection, full of wisdom and perfect in beauty. You were in Eden, the garden of God; every precious stone was your covering, sardius, topaz, and diamond, beryl, onyx, and jasper, sapphire, emerald, and carbuncle; and crafted in gold were your settings and your engravings. On the day that you were created they were prepared. You were an anointed guardian cherub. I placed you; you were on the holy mountain of God; in the midst of the stones of fire you walked. - Ezekiel 28:11-16

From these verses, we learn that this angel (cherub) was created in perfection and beauty. He was a high ranking, if not the highest ranking of the angelic host (the guardian cherub). God gave this beautiful, perfect angel a very special place in His presence, "in the midst of the stones of fire he walked." This description suggests the "son of dawn" had unparalleled access to God's throne "on the holy mountain of God."

Notice also that this angel was present in Eden. However, it seems he made his appearance in Eden only after his fall from heaven. Ezekiel continues:

> You were blameless in your ways from the day you were created, till unrighteousness was found in you. In the abundance of your trade you were filled with violence in your midst, and you sinned; so I cast you as a profane thing from the mountain of God, and I destroyed you, O guardian cherub, from the midst of the stones of fire. Your heart was proud because of your beauty; you corrupted your wisdom for the sake of your splendor. I cast you to the ground. - Ezekiel 28:17-18

This beautiful, powerful angel, who stood closest to God in heaven, became proud because of his immense beauty (v.16). In pursuit of his own glory, he left his proper place as a worshiper and sought to be worshiped (v. 17). Isaiah confirms:

> You said in your heart, "I will ascend to heaven; above the stars of God I will set my throne on high; I will sit on the mount of assembly in the far reaches of the north; I will ascend above the heights of the clouds; I will make myself like the Most High." - Isaiah 14:13-14

Because Lucifer tried to become like God, apparently expecting to be worshiped as God, God cast him out of heaven (Ezekiel 28:17), together with one-third of the angels who followed his rebellion (Revelation 12:4). Though he was hurled from heaven to the earth, he, now God's adversary, remained a spiritual being of immense beauty and power, who was attractive to Adam and Eve and obviously very persuasive in Eden.

So Satan (the devil) is a fallen angel and the leader of fallen angels (demons), who oppose God's purposes and people. He operates as a deceiver, which is why Jesus called him the "father of lies" (John 8:44). In other words, evil began with the devil.

Jesus dealt directly with Satan and his demons throughout his life and ministry. He spoke about them to His disciples and to them when He rebuked them. He confronted demons and cast them out of those whom they oppressed, even as He taught about their war against God and the way they tempt people to sin.

Because the most common biblical usage of "serpent" refers to literal, physical snakes, and because in Genesis 3, God curses the serpent by saying he would "be on his belly...," many assume the serpent in Eden was a snake, or perhaps a snake indwelled by the devil. But the text does not say this explicitly. It simply describes the serpent as being "craftier than all the beasts of the field." This phrase may just be a comparison to the beasts of the field, not a declaration that this serpent was one of these beasts (i.e., a snake).

When God cursed the devil by implying he would lick the dust in defeat, God was pointing to the ultimate judgment he would bring on the devil for deceiving Eve and tempting Adam to rebel against Him in Eden.

Finally, it's instructive to see that the sin which

caused Satan to fall from heaven was the very sin he tempted Adam and Eve to commit—to put themselves in the place of God. As this rebellion ruined the great angel and ejected Him from God's presence, the same happened to Adam and Eve. The difference is that God would redeem mankind. But the devil and his demons were hardened in their rebellion and forever judged as the enemies of God.

Was God Tempting Adam and Eve With the Tree?

So why did God place the tree of the knowledge of good and evil in the Garden of Eden in the first place? Wasn't He just setting Adam and Eve up to fail by tempting them to eat the tree's fruit? To answer the first and larger question of why God planted the tree in the garden, we must first understand that there was nothing magical or special about the tree itself. It was just a beautiful fruit tree that God created and, subsequently, selected to use for greater purposes.

He could have just as easily called Adam and Eve to stay out of the garden pond, or to never pet the garden llama. More importantly, even if God hadn't have given them any "don't eat, touch, etc." commands, Adam and Eve might still have rebelled against Him, because rebellion is, fundamentally, a matter of the heart.

Simply put, God's point in giving the first couple a forbidden tree was to remind them that He was God and they were not. Thriving as human beings created in the image of God would require that they/we stay personally and fully submitted to Him. God was not tempting Adam and Eve with the tree, nor did the presence of the tree cause their rebellion. Instead, God placed the tree in the garden out of kindness to Adam's race, as a perpetual, public reminder and warning, that we were made to live under Him, in full submission to Him.

The decision the first humans made to eat from the tree was, at its core, a heart decision to usurp God's throne by trying to make themselves equal with Him—an absurd but alluring temptation from the serpent that ultimately destroyed them and their race. We saw in the last toggle that the serpent made the same fateful choice when, as the archangel of God, He tried to usurp God's throne. He too received the just and practical penalty for his foolishness—he was ejected from God's presence.

Hoping to drag Adam and Eve into his misery, the serpent enticed them to become discontent with paradise. They believed his lies and turned away from God, expressing the rebellion in their hearts by eating the forbidden fruit. But the tree and its fruit were only the means through which

Adam and Eve exercised their defiance. The tree of the knowledge of good and evil was not the cause of their rebellion. They were the cause of their rebellion, as they willfully sought to be like God.

Chapter 7

Defying Gravity

I was seven years old and in the second grade, standing at the bus stop, waiting with the neighbor kids for our ride to school. One of my friends started telling me how his dad could make him flip, and how much fun it was.

"Yeah," he said, "it's easy. I just put my hands through my legs like this." He bent over and pushed his hands, front to back, through his legs at the knees. "Then my dad stands behind me and pulls my hands so I flip. Wanna try it?"

Of course I did. What seven-year-old boy doesn't want to flip in the air?

My friend, who was my height (a very important variable in this equation), stood behind me as I pushed my hands through my legs at the knees. "Okay, I said, "I'm ready."

My little friend grabbed my hands and yanked

as hard as he could. But instead of flipping me in the air, he face-planted me into the sidewalk, knocking me out cold.

I remember sudden darkness, flashes of light and then nothing. The next thing I knew, I was throwing up at home with a cartoon-sized knob on my forehead.

It took me several years to figure out exactly what went wrong that day. Turns out my friend had miscalculated his ability to get me high enough off the ground to flip me. And it seems we both underestimated the power of gravity that ensured my head would hit the ground with a brutal thud.

But I've never been tempted to *blame* gravity for that knot on my head. It wasn't gravity's *fault* I hit the ground. Gravity simply did what gravity does.

The same principle is true in the spiritual realm. Spiritual gravity anchors us to God and holds us right-side-up as we submit to Him. Or, it flips us upside-down and face-plants us when we rebel against Him. The fall of man in Eden was like my face-plant on the sidewalk. When we rebelled against God, we knocked ourselves spiritually and morally unconscious, which means we lost the ability to do anything truly good.

We Can't do Anything Good?

No wonder our world is full of evil and suffering. We are spiritually and morally incapacitated. Only the shadow of a conscience that God sustains in us keeps us from hitting the bottom of the slide and destroying ourselves and one another completely.

Understanding the devastating effects of our fall in Eden was helpful to my friend Johnny as he thought about our world's brokenness and our need to rise from the fall. But he struggled to understand, as many of us do, why the effects of the fall were so drastic. Did it really have to be this bad? Couldn't God have made His point about sin without allowing evil on earth to get so out of hand?

This led Johnny, Dave and me into one of the toughest questions we face as human beings. "Why does life hurt so much?" Why do relationships go bad? Why does disease poison our lives and kill the ones we love? Why do bad guys win and good guys lose? Why do babies suffer, rapists go free, dreams disappoint, parents fail and kids hate mom and dad? Without a doubt, what surprises me most about life is how much it hurts.

Growing up, I was repeatedly assured that you and I are basically good and only one step from living happily ever after. With just a little more money, knowledge, religion, medicine or time, we could bring heaven to earth. Every Disney movie I watched reinforced this deception. If only we look deep enough within each person, goodness, hope and light will shine through, and one day compel us to stop leaving, abusing, cheating and betraying one another. In time, if we worked together, we would cure all diseases and make suffering a thing of the past. We would live happily ever after.

Such a nice story. One I wish was true. But like the enchanted forest or the "happily ever after" bliss of a Disney prince and princess, this story is a myth. The truth is much harder to take.

Sooner or later, we must deal with the reality that the deeper we look into ourselves, the more we see why "happily ever after" is forever beyond our reach—not because of someone else, but because of *us*. We are not mere victims groping in the dark. You and I, *we* are the darkness. *We* are the brokenness in our broken world. *We* are the culprits and the victims, the abused and the abusers. Unable to escape our darkness, we sabotage the happily ever after we long for.

But even if we have the courage to admit this, we struggle to fathom why there is *so much* evil in the world. The intensity and amount of seemingly unnecessary suffering can make us wonder what God is doing. Is He in control or not?

If he's in control, why doesn't He intervene and make things right? Maybe He wants to make things right, but He lacks the power to do so. Or, as my daughter Trea asked me, "What if God is a tyrant?" What if God is all powerful but He isn't really good? The answers to these questions profoundly shape the story we find ourselves in, so we must have the courage to face them.

I've found I must approach the problem of evil *logically* and *existentially*. My logic asks why there is evil in the world at all. The existential (intuitive) part of me asks, "How can I live as if God is good and in control when so many suffer so deeply?"

Regarding the logical problem of evil, it's important to remember that goodness is, by definition, the way things are meant to be. As we've seen, the essence of goodness flows from the nature of God Himself, so that He is the source of life as it ought to be. That's why, when we are rightly connected to God, we experience *shalom*.

Because Adam and Eve were rightly connected to God in Eden, they began with a clear sense of identity, vision and purpose. But they learned the hard way that when we stop worshiping God to worship ourselves, we lose the center and source of goodness.

Think about a bicycle wheel. If you disconnected the spokes from the center hub, they could not bear your weight. If you tried to ride the bike, the spokes would immediately bend, twist and collapse. And then gravity would throw you to the ground.

In the same way, because we are disconnected from God (our hub), the spokes of our lives and world have warped, twisted and collapsed underneath us. No wonder our world is broken, careening out of control and ruined by spiritual gravity.

But this isn't God's fault or failure. We're broken because we broke away from Him. And the effects of our rebellion are disastrous. Remember, God made us in His image to make consequential decisions that reach beyond ourselves and affect our world.

Isn't this the power of self-determination we desire? Don't we want to make decisions that impact our world? What if we really have this much dignity, power and responsibility? What if the impact of our choices really is this significant?

The hard truth is, our fall in Eden disconnected us from the source and center of goodness. That disconnect twisted our identity and turned our world upside-down and inside-out. Because we're sinners by nature and by choice, our world is dominated by the way things should *not* be. But this is the nature of evil (non-good), the consequence of our rebellion against God.

Why Did Adam's Sin Ruin Me?

If you're like me, you find this explanation logically helpful but emotionally unsatisfying. After all, understanding the cause of their suffering won't comfort the grieving parents of a child killed in an accident, or the victim of a tsunami, rape or personal betrayal. That's because evil isn't just a concept to be explained; it's a painful reality we must endure. Evil is an ugly part of the story we find ourselves in. We see evil in ourselves, face it in others and watch it contort the very fabric of our world. Evil invades our lives relentlessly through disease, disasters and relational suffering, as we endure intensely personal encounters with the way things should not be.

Surely the ancient story, if it matches our deepest yearnings, will lead us through our encounters with evil and engage our hope that evil will one day be swallowed up forever. I explained to Johnny and Dave that finding God in the midst of evil is the key to finding this hope, because I'm convinced that God is, as He claims to be in the Bible, all powerful *and* perfectly good. He isn't the cause of evil and He grieves over the suffering evil causes—so much so that, as we will see, God chose to be crushed by evil in order to conquer it forever.

In addition, He promises to execute perfect and final justice when He restores shalom to the earth at the end of the age.[27] Knowing these things at least allows me to give God the benefit of the

27 See for example, Revelation 19:11-21; 2 Peter 3:9-13

doubt when I cannot understand why this or that evil event takes place.

Taking it a step further, I actually believe that God *uses* evil to point us to Himself. Let me explain by asking some questions.

Which would be more loving, for God to cover up the effects of the fall so that we don't recognize our need for rescue, or for Him to allow us to experience the pain of our broken world, so that we turn to Him and point our world to Him for healing?

What if the effects of our rebellion are far worse than we'll ever understand? Could it be that our world isn't nearly as bad as it might be if God truly let the evil within us run rampant?

What if God's goodness is intervening and protecting us from the unthinkable darkness our evil is capable of? What if we deserve eternal judgment for our rebellion, in addition to the full weight of the evil we've unleashed upon ourselves? But what if, as bad as our experiences with evil may be, they are only a fraction of what we deserve them to be?

Could it be that God's goodness brings us face to face with our evil *and* protects us from the full weight of evil that we deserve for our rebellion against Him? I believe so. We see this reflected in the way God dealt with fallen man from the beginning. Even as God judged mankind for rebelling against Him, He promised to defy spiritual gravity for us, lift us from our fall, rekindle the fire within and teach us to sing again.

But defying the effects of spiritual gravity for us would require God to subject Himself to the destructive force of this gravity. Amazingly God voluntarily entered and suffered at evil's highest point to set us free from its bondage. Let's pick up the action in Genesis 3:15.

> So the LORD God said to the serpent, "Because you have done this, Cursed are you above all the livestock and all the wild animals! You will crawl on your belly and you will eat dust all the days of your life. And I will put enmity between you and the woman, and between your offspring and hers; **he will crush your head, and you will strike his heel**."[28]

Immediately before describing the curse we brought upon ourselves through sin, God promised to lift us from our tragic fall, to return us to

---

28 Genesis 3:15

life as it was meant to be with Him as our center. He does this by first cursing the serpent. In the process, He reveals His plan to personally secure our salvation at unspeakable cost to Himself.

We'll talk more about God's suffering at the hands of evil in Chapter Nine. For now, notice that God foretells a cosmic battle (enmity) between the offspring of Eve and that of the serpent. At first, it seems God is referring to all Eve's children (the human race). But look closely. In the second half of verse 15, God says "he," a single, male offspring from Eve, would one day crush the devil's head (destroy him forever). But Eve's seed, though wounded (bruised on the heel) by the enemy, would not be utterly destroyed.

Who is this male seed of the woman who would defeat the devil in battle? As the story unfolds throughout the Bible, it becomes increasingly clear that "he" is the promised Messiah, Jesus Christ—the one who came to "take away the sin of the world,"[29] by living a perfect life and dying a brutal, sacrificial death, to conquer sin and break us free from its destructive grasp.

29 John 1:29

As we'll see in Chapter Nine, Jesus Christ wasn't just a man. He was and is *God who became flesh*—fully God and fully man, the one and only God-man. But if the promised Messiah is God in human flesh, then, in Genesis 3:15, God promised to *personally* subject Himself to the height of evil in order to conquer it.

Out of love for us, God promised to enter the crushing vortex of the black hole called sin, to reverse the effects of the fall, turn us right-side out and reenergize our fallen souls to shine again in His presence. God's vulnerable pursuit of mankind is staggering—and the central theme of the story we find ourselves in.

So, regarding evil in our world, I believe God, in His goodness, makes us face the evil that flows from our sin, even as He protects us from the full weight of the evil we deserve for our sin. And, ultimately, God promised to enter and conquer evil by conquering sin, evil and death as our Messiah.

Knowing these things helps me greatly in dealing with the reality of evil in my world. Though I may not always understand what He's doing or why He allows certain things to happen, I can rest in the proven knowledge that God is good and all powerful, and that He has broken the back of evil.

Moreover, according to His ancient promise, a day is coming when evil will no longer find a place on earth. So I can say to those who are suffering, "There is a God in heaven who sees and hates your pain. He has acted in history at great personal cost to destroy the source of your pain. He will comfort your pain in this life. And one day, pain will be no more, because evil will be devoured."

We Can't do Anything Good?

Evil is the absence of good. It is non-good—a negative, not a positive quality. Evil is the way things ought not to be, because they are not functioning as they should be. As darkness is the absence of light, evil is the absence of good. As the hole in the center of the donut is the lack of donut, evil is the lack of good.

Because God is perfectly and necessarily good, He could not be the cause of evil, nor be corrupted by evil. God created Adam and Eve perfectly good. But they were not *necessarily* good. In other words, unlike God, they were corruptible. Though they began morally perfect, evil *could* make them less than perfectly good.

When Adam and Eve sinned, their nature was corrupted by evil. They became what they were not meant to be. The light within them faded, as sin darkened every part of their intellect, emotions and will. Had God not intervened to preserve some sense of a moral conscience within them, they would have destroyed themselves completely.

History and scripture reveal man's intractable tendency toward destructive evil (see Romans 1:18-32). Though God, in His grace, has sustained a conscience within us (Romans 2:12-16), the Prophet Isaiah reminds us that even our most righteous deeds are stained with sin, so that nothing we do is truly good. Because of the fall, our motives are always mixed (Isaiah 64:6). We can only do "good," relative to that which is less good. We are incapable of doing anything truly good, so as to earn God's favor or claim ultimate moral superiority over others.

We don't want to believe this. We'd like to think we are basically good. But when we inventory the evil thoughts, motives and desires that lurk just below the surface of our facades, we are forced to admit that we are fallen and broken, in desperate need of forgiveness, grace and ongoing renewal. The good news is that God knows our need and has made a way for us to return to Eden and (ultimately) moral perfection with Him.

Why Did Adam's Sin Ruin Me?

It's easy to understand how Adam and Eve ruined themselves by rebelling against God. It's more difficult to grasp how and why their sin ruined us. But the Bible teaches that Adam's sin plunged the entire human race under the curse of sin, so that we are sinners from birth, in need of rescue by the promised Messiah who has come (Jesus Christ). In the words of the Apostle Paul:

> Therefore, just as sin came into the world through one man, and death through sin, and so death spread to all men because all sinned [in Adam]... death reigned from Adam to Moses, even over those whose sinning was not like the transgression of Adam, who was a type of the one who was to come. (Romans 5:12-14 ESV)

> For as in Adam all die, so also in Christ shall all be made alive. (1 Corinthians 15:22 ESV)

King David concurs:

> Behold, I was brought forth in iniquity, and in sin did my mother conceive me. (Psalm 51:5 ESV)

Three realities help me understand how Adam's sin could ruin me. Let's consider each in turn.

1. Our connectedness as a race. We who have been shaped by Western individualism tend to struggle with a robust view of solidarity within the human race. Eastern thinkers are less troubled with the notion that all human beings are deeply connected, and that our choices affect one another significantly.

In the same way, many of us bristle at the idea of someone speaking for us and determining our destiny. But much of the world has lived under this reality throughout history. For example, a king had (has) the power to make treaties that his people must defend. A king can surrender his people to an enemy, even relegate them to slavery as part of the terms of surrender. This is because the king is the head of his people and, therefore, their legal representative. The king acts on behalf of his subjects who are legally bound by his edicts and actions.

As the head of the human race, Adam was our legal representative. As his race, our destiny was inextricably tied to his decisions. Adam was charged with leading us forward to fill the earth with God's glory by walking in submission to God in paradise. But Adam rebelled against God, casting himself, and us, under the curse of sin. Though Eve participated with Adam in the fall, it was the actions of Adam (the head and legal representative of our race) that enslaved us. This is why the verses above refer to our fall with Adam, not Eve.

We may not like the fact that Adam had the legal authority to represent us in this way. But we must not confuse our notion of fairness with ultimate justice. In a legal sense, Adam was our representative, our spokesman and head. He had the legal right and responsibility to act on our behalf, and we bear the consequences of his actions. He led us into slavery to sin. We became slaves to sin with him, our head.

2. Our genetic presence with Adam in Eden. When God created Adam, He created the entire human race in Him. God drew from Adam's humanity (physically and spiritually) to create Eve. Together, Adam and Eve propagated our common humanity throughout the earth. We are all offspring of Adam, by definition.

Obviously, as the genetic head of the human race, Adam played a unique and powerful role in human history. After all, you and I were present with Adam in Eden, in the sense that the humanity we now exemplify came directly from him. We get our physical and spiritual DNA from Adam because he is our most ancient ancestor.

All of us affect others in the human race by our choices. But Adam's power over our race was unique in at least two ways. First, his choices would affect the spiritual and physical make-up of every human being who would ever live (with the possible exception of Eve, but she sinned with Adam and ruined herself along with him).

Second, given the far reaching consequences of Adam's choice to rebel against God, this choice was the most profound and consequential decision in human history.

When Adam disconnected himself from the source of life, we became disconnected with him. His entire nature as a human being was deeply scarred by his fall, so that all his posterity would inherit bodies and souls filled with brokenness and death. Adam's race fell with him, and we are his race.

3. My intuition that I have always had a sinful nature. My intellectual angst over how Adam's sin made me a sinner recedes when I honestly consult my intuitions. Deep down, I know I am fallen, broken and guilty before God. I've known this for as long as I've known anything. I wonder if you know this about yourself as well.

Aren't we all aware that things on Planet Earth aren't as they should be? And, if the truth be told, don't we know that we are part of the problem? In our most candid moments, we know we are sinners by nature and by choice. With King David, I can say, "Behold, I was brought forth in iniquity, and in sin did my mother conceive me." I know I inherited a fallen nature at conception. But I also know that, no matter how this happened, I am personally culpable for who I am. I know that I have ratified and voluntarily owned my fallen nature through countless evil choices throughout my life. Deep down, I know I am deeply broken and in desperate need of renewal. I cannot blame anyone for who I am. I need redemption. What about you?

Chapter 8

A River Runs Through It

I grew up in Boise, Idaho, which means I grew up enjoying the Boise River. The city of Boise has been shaped by the river that shares its name for almost 150 years.

Rivers have played this role throughout human history and provide a beautiful analogy for history itself. You could say there is an ancient "river" running through humanity that unites and shapes us all. This river is the story of our creation and fall from Eden, our search for lost shalom and God's unfolding promise to take us back to Eden through His Messiah, the Christ.

Seeing how God's plan has unfolded throughout history gives me confidence He will fulfill His promises in the future. So let's consider pivotal moments in the past where God has shaped our story through decisive steps to take us back to Eden.

Following Adam and Eve and many, many generations of their descendants, the book of *Genesis* introduces us to a man named, Abraham,[30] who lived some 4,100 years ago. God chose Abraham to father a nation that would bring His Messiah, our rescuer, into the world.

Expanding on His promise to Adam and Eve in Genesis 3, the Lord said to Abraham,

> "...Go from your country and your kindred and your father's house to the **land** that I will show you. And I will make of you a great **nation**, and I will bless you and make your name great, so that you will be a blessing. I will bless those who bless you, and him who dishonors you I will curse, and **in you all the families of the earth shall be blessed**."[31]

God promised Abraham that the **nation** which would come from him would dwell in the promised **land**. As the details unfold, we discover this is the Land of Canaan, also known as Palestine. Pretty straight forward.

30 Initially, his name was Abram. But God eventually changed his name to Abraham. I will refer to him only as "Abraham" here to avoid confusion.

31 Genesis 15:1-3

But check out the last line in this promise. God tells Abraham that *all* nations (everyone, including you and me) would be **blessed** through him. How could Abraham bless all people in every generation? By being the father of the people, through whom would come the Messiah, who would lift us from the fall and renew all things.

God expands His promise to Abraham in *Genesis* 17 and extends it to Abraham's son, Isaac, and to his grandson, Jacob.[32] Along the way, God changed Jacob's name to "Israel." The *man*, Israel, had twelve sons who fathered the twelve tribes of the nation of Israel, through whom would come the Christ.

A few more details are helpful. *Genesis* records that the Pharaoh of Egypt invited Israel's family to live in Egypt during a famine around 1870 B.C. But within a few generations, Egypt turned against Israel (also called the "Jews") and made them their slaves. For nearly four-hundred years, Israel multiplied in Egypt until the Egyptians began to fear them, and the Pharaoh ordered the execution of all Jewish baby boys in an attempt to

32 See Genesis 26-28

weaken the Jewish nation.

At this time, around 1526 B.C., a Jewish slave-boy named Moses was born. I call your attention to the story of Moses and Israel in Egypt, because it marks another pivotal moment in God's plan to lift us from our fall and take us back to Eden.

Through an unusual turn of events, the baby Moses was adopted by Pharaoh's daughter, who raised Moses in the palace, as the older stepbrother of one who was to become the next Pharaoh. This Pharaoh-to-be probably saw Moses as a threat and would have been eager to get rid of him.

One day, after Moses was an adult and his stepbrother had become Pharaoh, Moses defended a fellow Jew against the violence of an Egyptian. This was an insult to the Egyptians who ruled the Jews, so Moses' stepbrother- pharaoh ordered Moses' arrest and execution. But Moses fled into the wilderness, where, for forty years, he endured an obscure life as a fugitive.

Finally, after Moses' stepbrother-pharaoh died and another took the throne, God called Moses to return to Egypt to set His people (the Jews) free from slavery.

Leveraging his knowledge of Egyptian law and culture, and miraculous intervention by God, Moses convinced the new Pharaoh to release the Jews from slavery. Moses led them out of Egypt, through the desert and into the promised land of Canaan. Check out the crazy details in *Exodus*, the second book of the Bible.

The story of Moses and the rescue of Israel out of Egypt is an example of God's persistent intervention in history to lift us from the fall and take us back to Eden. As we saw earlier, the children of Abraham, who became the nation of Israel, played a key role in God's plan to bring His Messiah to our rescue.

Having led the nation of Israel to the doorstep of the land God had promised them through Abraham, Moses wanted to make sure the Jews understood their crucial place in God's story. So he took them back to the beginning, by writing the narrative in what we know today as the first five books of the Bible.

As we saw in chapters six and seven, Moses began by telling of the God who was there before anything else—the One who created all things, especially man, whom He made in His image. Moses told of the serpent, the fall of Adam and Eve and the tragedy of the curse. Most importantly, He spoke of God's promised Messiah who would one day conquer the power of sin, reverse the effects of the fall and restore the shalom of Eden.

Throughout the rest of *Genesis*, Moses reminded the Jews God had chosen them to reveal Himself and bring His Christ into the world through them. He wanted them to understand their heritage so they would embrace their destiny.

Now, how does all this history apply to you and me today? As I explained to Johnny and Dave, the story of Israel is at the heart of the story we find ourselves in. God's plan to lift you and me from the fall meant raising up and preserving the Jewish nation, through whom would come the Messiah, the Savior of the world.

Back in chapter two, we talked about how the story that brings the pieces of life together would satisfy our core intuitions and make sense of the human condition as a whole. And we agreed it would need to be deeply embedded in history to apply to all people. Well, *this* is *that* story—the river that flows through our history, and the way God fulfilled His promise to lift us from our fall.

The rest of the Old Testament reveals God's continually unfolding plan to make all things new through His coming Messiah, the Christ. For example, through Moses, God established ceremonies and a sacrificial system that foreshadowed what the Christ would do to break the power of evil and make us new.

After Moses, the Prophets, who spanned more than a thousand years between 1500-400 B.C., predicted the lineage, birthplace, characteristics and mission of the Messiah to come.[33]

During the period of these prophets, in about 1000 B.C., God chose a man named David to be king over Israel. Like Abraham and Moses before Him, David was a pivotal figure in the unfolding drama we find ourselves in. This is because, by God's design, King David's dominant reign on the earth foreshadowed the kingly, *universal* reign of the Christ to come.

More than that, after being chosen by God to build the nation of Israel into the envy of the

---

33 See for example, 2 Samuel 7:11-17; Psalm 72:10; Isaiah 7:14, 9:1-6, 53; Micah 5:2

world, King David received a stunning promise from God:

> ...I will give you rest from all your enemies. Moreover, the LORD declares to you that the LORD will make you a house. When your days are fulfilled and you lie down with your fathers, I will raise up your offspring after you, who shall come from your body, and I will establish his kingdom. He shall build a house for my name, and **I will establish the throne of his kingdom forever**.[34]

Eleven-hundred years after promising Abraham that the Messiah would come through His line and make all things new, God told David, Abraham's descendent, that his (David's) kingdom would never end. But only God's Kingdom is everlasting. So, by promising David that *his* (David's) kingdom would never end, God was promising David that the Messiah would come through his line and establish God's everlasting Kingdom on earth. For this reason, "Son of David" became a popular way of referring to the coming Messiah.

Roughly one-thousand years after God made

---

34 2 sam. 7:11-13

this promise to David, the "Son of David" (Messiah) came to fulfill God's ancient promise to take us back to Eden and teach us to sing again. We are finally ready to take a closer look at the Champion of our story.

Chapter 9

X-Man

It was a warm summer night in San Antonio, Texas. I was six-years old. My brothers were seven and eight. Mom and dad were out for the evening, so we had a babysitter who spent most of her time inside the house with my three-year-old sister, Elizabeth.

After watching "The Green Berets," a John Wayne classic about the Vietnam War, we three boys headed outside.

In the backyard, we talked about our fascination with the scene in the movie where soldiers jumped from an airplane and their parachutes deployed automatically. One thing led to another, and soon we were climbing onto the roof of the playhouse (something we weren't allowed to do when mom and dad were home). Though the playhouse wasn't more than twelve-feet tall, climbing to the top felt like quite a feat.

Once we were standing on the roof, one of my brothers suggested I jump off. "Your parachute will open automatically," he assured me.

"Yeah," the other agreed quickly, "It'll open automatically."

This seemed reasonable enough to me. After all, I'd just seen it done in the movie, so I decided it was worth a shot. Without hesitation, I moved to the edge, looked over and jumped. My parachute didn't open, because, of course, I wasn't wearing one. Not surprisingly, I slammed into the ground and broke my foot. We didn't know my foot was broken at first, but we did know my limp would require a cover story for the sitter, and more importantly, for Mom and Dad.

We made it to bed without incident. However, in the morning, it was impossible to hide my swollen, multi-colored foot. All three of us (and my foot) were busted.

I really wanted to be like a Green Beret that night. They were the heroes of the movie. What young boy doesn't want to be a hero?

In the years to come, I would imagine myself as all sorts of heroes. What I lacked in good sense, I made up for in imagination. For example, I often pretended to be the only survivor of a bloody military battle. Wounded (usually shot through the shoulder), I'd struggle to fight off my invisible enemy just in time for reinforcements to arrive. I was amazing.

Like any kid, I was lured by super heroes as well. For me, the most impressive hero (though the tights always troubled me) was Superman. Man of Steel. Faster than a speeding bullet. And he could fly! But what really impressed me about Superman was the way he defended justice, and consistently conquered the forces of evil. My kind of guy.

What about you? Who was your favorite superhero? Better yet, who are your real life heroes? Perhaps a parent or teacher, a political or revolutionary leader, a soldier, inventor or renowned problem-solver?

The greater our needs and the more powerless we feel, the more we look for champions to advance our causes. The more we encounter the evil and injustice that poisons our world, the more we long for someone who will make things right.

But even our heroes leave us wanting, because, at best, they only deal with the *symptoms* of evil, one at a time. What we really need is a champion who will vanquish evil once and for all, who will deal with the depth and source of our brokenness and make all things new.

History reveals our continual tendency to hate, abuse and destroy one another, reminding us of our deep brokenness and inability to rescue ourselves. We are in desperate need of an enduring hero—a Messiah. We long for the Savior that God promised to Adam and Eve, Abraham, Moses, David and the prophets.

I'm convinced Jesus is this Messiah, the culmination of God's plan to crush the curse, lift us from the fall, and teach us to sing again. Jesus claimed to be God's Messiah and He wrapped His words in actions only the Messiah could perform.

Jesus had a humble beginning and a normal, first-century, Jewish childhood. But all that changed when he stood up in an ancient synagogue and read a well-known passage from the Prophet Isaiah about God's coming Messiah. His reading of this scripture wasn't controversial. But when He told the crowd that *He* was the fulfillment of Isaiah's prophecy (that He was the long-awaited Messiah), the fireworks began.

His ninety-second sermon astonished the Jewish leaders and launched a revolution that's still rocking our world today. *He* had come to reverse the effects of the fall and conquer the power of sin, to inaugurate God's spiritual Kingdom on earth and take us back to the future we lost in Eden.

Listen to what Jesus said about Himself that day:

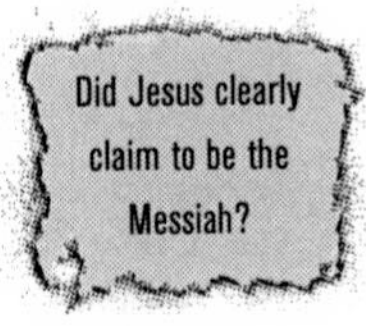

Did Jesus clearly
claim to be the
Messiah?

> Jesus... stood up to read. And the scroll of the prophet Isaiah was given to him. He unrolled the scroll and found the place where it was written, "The Spirit of the Lord is upon me, because he has anointed me to proclaim **good news to the poor**. He has sent me to proclaim **liberty to the captives** and **recovery of sight to the blind, to set at liberty those who are oppressed**, to proclaim the **year of the Lord's favor**."
>
> And he rolled up the scroll and gave it back to the attendant and sat down. And the eyes of all in the synagogue were fixed on him. And he began to say to them, "**Today this Scripture has been fulfilled in your hearing.**"[35]

35 Luke 4:16-21 Isaiah 61:1-2

Faithful Jews had waited more than two-thousand years for Isaiah's prophecy to be fulfilled. They knew that only the Messiah could proclaim the "year of the Lord's favor," as Jesus had done.

By applying Isaiah's prophecy to Himself, Jesus was claiming that God's promise had been fulfilled in Him; that He, the promised Messiah, had come.

The religious elite were understandably skeptical of His declaration. Many were offended. A mob even tried to kill Jesus for implying that day that He was the Messiah.[36] But Jesus escaped their grasp and began proving by His actions that He was, in fact, the Christ they had been looking for.

Jesus' relationship with the Jewish religious leaders would never be friendly. Turns out they were looking for a Messiah made in their own image, someone to bolster *their* traditions, power and goals.

They despised Jesus' lack of sophistication and unsavory habit of hanging around the outcasts of society. But those who were unworthy of the religious establishment, it seems, were the ones Jesus sought most to rescue from the fall.

---

36 Luke. 4:22-30

But isn't rescuing people exactly what Isaiah prophesied the Messiah would do? He would lift up those devastated by the fall, reverse the effects of the curse and bring hope to all people. He would inaugurate God's Kingdom on earth.

By loving, healing and transforming those in most obvious need of renewal, Jesus compels us to see ourselves in them and admit we've all been ruined by the fall. He calls us to see that we're all outcasts of Eden, in desperate need of a do-over, a new beginning, new life.

Through His exemplary life, Jesus reminded us how we once lived when we were connected to the source of life, and how things will be again when God's Kingdom fills the earth. His actions spoke as loudly as His words.

Do the Gospels Record the Actual Words of Jesus?

Jesus showed compassion to the poor

Jesus' words are recorded in the New Testament Gospels (Matthew, Mark, Luke and John). He spoke often *about* the poor, *to* the poor, and called His disciples to *care* for the poor. He insisted that His genuine followers would do the same, and that those who neglected the hungry, thirsty and naked could not claim to be His.[37]

On two occasions, Jesus fed the masses (many of whom were poor) by miraculously multiplying bread and fish to feed thousands at a time. In addition, He called the poor "blessed"[38] because, unlike the wealthy and comfortable who deluded themselves into thinking all was well, the poor clearly grasped the brokenness of our world and their need for rescue.

Jesus saw their pain and had compassion for them. He offered them spiritual renewal in this life, and a new creation at the end of the age, when poverty would be less than a memory. He taught His disciples to feed and clothe the poor as a down-payment on this certain future with Him.[39]

Jesus liberated the oppressed

They were infected with a contagious, flesh-eating disease called leprosy. Nobody wanted to touch a leper for fear of catching this horrible plague. Lepers were unwanted, rejected and rel-

37 Matthew 25:31-45

38 Luke 6:20-23

39 See for example, Matthew 25:31-40

egated to a life of isolation and shame. Forced to remove themselves from society, they had to shout "unclean" to all who approached them.

While the Law of Moses initiated the quarantine of lepers to protect the larger community, it was never God's intent for the leper to be shunned, shamed or dehumanized. But this is what ultimately happened.

Imagine people running away at the sight of you, or longing for loved ones to touch you, but experiencing only rejection and scorn. The loneliness and desperation would be overwhelming, because we were made for relationship, love and touch.

Lepers were often treated (and surely felt) as if they were sub-human. Not allowed to connect with others, they were expected to die in isolation. Out of sight. Out of the way. Untouchable.

But Jesus refused to allow their disease to define them. Instead, to the surprise of all, Jesus loved the lepers of His day by *touching* them to heal them.[40] He saw their disease for what it was, a consequence of the fall. And He saw lepers as they truly were, people created in God's image and deeply valu-

40 See for example, Matthew 8:1-3

able to Him. Jesus came to conquer the fall and its effects, to offer every person love, respect and touch, regardless of how the fall affects them.

Jesus consistently stood in the gap for the vulnerable and abused. For example, in first-century Palestine, women were at the bottom of the social scale. They had few rights, were often treated as property, and a woman's testimony was invalid in court.

But Jesus defended the value of women as equal to men and restored their dignity in society by befriending them, eating with them, and inviting them to follow Him. This behavior was highly unusual. Jewish rabbis (teachers) did not associate with women in public.

But Jesus wasn't your average rabbi. He not only involved women in His ministry, He allowed them into His inner circle. And, most remarkably, after His resurrection from the dead, Jesus appeared to His female disciples before He appeared to His male apostles.[41] He could have done nothing greater to restore the God-given status of women in a society that oppressed them.

Jesus treated all human beings with dignity be-

41 Matthew 28:1-10

cause they were created in God's image and were, therefore, valuable to Him. He even went out of His way to dignify children. In one instance, when kids were running to be with Him, his disciples rebuked them and told these children not to bother Jesus. But Jesus surprised them by inviting the children to come to Him, to enjoy Him, to feel their worth.[42]

Setting us free from the oppression of the fall, Jesus showed us how to live and treat one another with dignity and honor, regardless of our status or station in life, simply because we are human beings—God's image bearers.

Jesus broke down walls of prejudice

Remember how Adam and Eve became distant from one another after becoming alienated from God? Once they lost their vertical relationship with Him, their community with one another began to suffer as they began distrusting, blaming and suspecting one another.

Unfortunately, this mistrust became the pattern for fallen mankind. Just look at our history. Rath-

42 Matthew 19:13-15

er than celebrate our common humanity under God, we divide into groups that malign, blame and suspect one another. Instead of embracing and enjoying our ethnic and cultural differences, we tend toward racism, bigotry and hate.

This animosity was true in Jesus' day as well. One of the sharpest divides in first-century Palestine was between Jews and Samaritans. Everybody knew that the Jews hated the Samaritans and the Samaritans despised the Jews. They had historical, cultural and religious reasons for their shared disdain, but none of their excuses were good enough for Jesus. For He had come to inaugurate God's Kingdom on earth, which is, at its core, a kingdom of peace; peace with God that produces peace with one another.

In one instance, He went out of His way to travel through Samaria, the land of the dreaded Samaritans.[43] His Jewish disciples couldn't understand why he would pollute His and their feet with Samaritan dust. On top of that, while in Samaria, Jesus talked with a Samaritan woman. Remember that women endured a very low stature

43 John 4:1-42

in that culture. But in a Jewish man's mind, *Samaritan* women were (if possible) even lower on the social scale than Jewish women.

To make matters worse, this Samaritan woman was openly sleeping around. As a result, she was a moral outcast, even among the despised Samaritans. But Jesus went out of His way to meet her, expose her brokenness, reveal himself as her Messiah and make her new.

After meeting Jesus and encountering the healing and hope only He could bring, the woman ran back to her village and told everyone about Him. Seeing the woman's transformation, the Samaritans invited Jesus to stay with them, which He did, overnight. The entire village discovered their Messiah and found new life in Him.

Jesus came to break down the walls that divide us, to become our unity and take us back to Eden-like community. He came to remind us that our value comes, not from our differences, but from our equality in the image of God. He came to renew our shared life as God's image bearers by offering the opportunity to find ourselves in Him, our common Savior.

Jesus performed miracles

Jesus often performed miracles to verify His identity and give us a taste of the Kingdom that had come—a spiritual Kingdom that would one day fill the earth. His miracles were never standalone events. They always revealed something about who Jesus is and what He came to do.

In His first miracle, Jesus turned 120 gallons of water into premium wine.[44] That amazing miracle told the story of why He had come—to transform us into something new. To invite us into the beauty, color and flavor of life as it was meant to be in Him.

Later, Jesus walked on water to proclaim His power over the creation He would one day restore.[45] He raised a friend from the dead to demonstrate His power over death.[46] And He cast out demons to prove He'd come to break the enduring grip that evil had on our world.[47] Jesus healed the sick, blind, deaf and lame to demonstrate *who* He was—Messiah, and *what* He had come to do—

---

44 John 2:1-12

45 Matthew 14:22-33

46 John 11:1-44

47 Mark 5:1-20

lift us from the fall and take us back to the shalom of Eden.

Jesus forgave sins

In one instance, Jesus healed a man born lame, even as He forgave the man's sins.[48] He did these things simultaneously to demonstrate His authority to conquer sin *and* its effects. All disease is a product of the fall in Eden. By exercising His power over the effects of the fall (this man's paralysis), Jesus proved He had authority to provide what this man (and we) need most, the forgiveness of sin.

The Prophet Isaiah's "favorable year of the Lord," which Jesus claimed to inaugurate, was, most of all, an offer of forgiveness to a rebellious world, a pardon for our sins, that we might enjoy peace with the God who made us to find our life in Him. This is why John the Baptist called Jesus "the lamb of God who takes away the sin of the world."[49] And this, more than anything else, is what makes Jesus our Champion—the only one

48 Mark 2:1-12

49 John 1:29

who can take us back to Eden.

I'll talk more about what this pardon means and how Jesus secured our forgiveness soon. For now, remember that our sin (rebellion against God) separates us from God, the source of life. Therefore, reconciling with God must be our highest priority, and forgiveness from God is our greatest need.

Jesus taught that sin is ultimately a matter of the heart.[50]

Whether we commit this or that evil deed, our rebellious hearts make us guilty before God and in need of His forgiveness.

Various cultures place special emphasis on certain sins and declare them particularly offensive, even unforgivable.

We often feel free to point a prideful finger at those we consider "sinners," as if we're better than them.

In Jesus day, the fingers pointed at prostitutes, tax-collectors (Jews working for the Romans to tax their Jewish brothers) and those who condoned such lifestyles. The religious elite went out of their

50 See for example, Matthew 5:21-30

way to avoid such filthy, shameful people.

Not surprisingly, Jesus took a different approach, which earned Him the title, "friend of sinners."[51] The religious leaders thought they were insulting Jesus with this nick-name, as they derided him for eating with, talking to and loving those whom they avoided. But Jesus saw this title as a badge of honor. For this is why He had come.

To be fair, if Jesus paid us a visit today and spent His time now as He did in the first century, many of today's religious leaders would be just as shocked by His actions as those first-century leaders were.

Today's leaders would be dumbfounded when He didn't attend their churches or rallies. They'd be dismayed by the time and energy He'd invest in broken people who could give Him nothing in return.

They'd be appalled by the places and events Jesus would frequent—crack houses, brothels and prisons, gay-pride parades, pro-choice and pro-life rallies, Wall Street, corporate board rooms and gyms. There we'd find Jesus, loving people and

51 Matthew 11:19

forgiving sins. He'd show up at hookah bars and local pubs, at Mardi Gras and fraternity rush.

Jesus would, today, as He did in the first century, meet people where they are, enjoy them as they are, and invite them to find new life in Him. With gang-bangers, potheads and girls-gone-wild, there we'd find our Messiah, the forgiver of our sin. Eventually, we'd understand that we're all in equal need of Him, and our elitist, moral pride simply betrays our darkened hearts.

The brokenness and sin of those who followed Jesus in the first century reminds me that He came to rescue people just like me. For example, Matthew was one of Jesus' twelve apostles and the writer of the "Gospel of Matthew." He was a pretty big deal. But get this. Matthew was a greedy tax-collector before he met Jesus. He was a despised traitor to his people, a selfish, money-grubbing scumbag who found forgiveness and new life in Jesus.

And don't forget those women caught in sexual sin. Jesus forgave them completely and invited them to begin again.

Did you know the Apostle Paul was a murderer of Christians before Jesus remade his heart and forgave his sins?[52] Or that the Apostle Peter publicly betrayed Jesus on the eve of His death, breaking Jesus' heart and leaving Him to suffer alone? Jesus forgave them both.

But most remarkable of all, Jesus forgave *me*. And He will forgive you, too. For this is why He came—to lift us from the fall, reconnect us with God and bring us certain hope that He will make us and all things new.

As we unfold His story, we'll watch Jesus voluntarily suffer evil at its highest point to conquer evil once and for all. Finally, we'll hear the resurrected Christ, our Hero and our Champion, say to all who come to Him, "My shalom I give to you."[53]

---

52 See Acts 7:54-58. "Saul" became "Paul" after His conversion to Jesus Christ in Acts 9.

53 John 20:19-26

Did Jesus Clearly Claim to be the Messiah?

Jesus knew He was the Messiah and referred to Himself as such through His words and His deeds. I listed many of His Messianic actions in this chapter. The following verbal assertions from Jesus show that He knew He was the Christ.

1. Jesus often referred to Himself as the "Son of Man" (e.g., Matthew 8:20, Mark 2:10). The Prophet Daniel used this title to identify the coming Messiah (Daniel 7:13-14). The Jews would have understood that Jesus was claiming to be the Messiah when He applied this title to Himself.

2. Jesus called Himself the "Son of God" (e.g., John 10:36). People knew this to be His central claim about Himself and often referred to Him in this way (e.g., John 20:31). Jesus' claim to be the Son of God compelled the Jews to crucify Him for blasphemy, because He claimed a unique relationship with God the Father that made Him equal with God (Matthew 27:40-44; John 5:18, 19:7). Moreover, the title, "Son of God," pointed to God's divine representative on the earth, to His

Messiah, the very "Son of Man" from Daniel 7. Taken together, the self-given titles, "Son of God" and "Son of Man" remove all doubt that Jesus believed He was the Messiah.

3. Jesus referred to Himself as the One the Old Testament scriptures pointed to (Luke 24:27). But those scriptures pointed to the Messiah. If Jesus was the object of Old Testament prophesy, He must be the Messiah.

4. Jesus claimed to be the only way to God (John 14:6). Every Jew knew that, ultimately, only the Messiah could make this assertion about Himself. Therefore, they would have understood that Jesus was declaring Himself to be the Messiah—our only way back to Eden.

5.Jesus affirmed Peter's assertion that He was the Messiah (Matthew 16:15-17).

6. Jesus explicitly referred to Himself as the Messiah while talking to the Samaritan woman in John 4 (John 4:26).

Do the Gospels Record the Actual Words of Jesus?

In addition to bibliographical analyses that confirm the historicity of the New Testament documents, there are many good reasons to believe the authors of the New Testament Gospels (Matthew, Mark, Luke and John) accurately and reliably recorded the historical life and words of Jesus. Several of those reasons are provided below.

1. The culture in which Jesus lived carried the expectation that the disciples of a rabbi would pay close attention to his words, so as to memorize and repeat them to others. Jesus' disciples apparently did just that. In the Gospels, they claimed to write history, not myth or legend, to record the very words and actions of Jesus. These documents (through their authors) implicitly and/or explicitly claimed to be historical—to record actual, historical words and events. As with any document of antiquity, the burden of proof rests with those who challenge the claims within a given document.

2. The literary genre of the Gospels is history, not myth or legend. All four books read like straightfor-

ward historical accounts, complete with gritty, unnecessary, and sometimes offensive and seemingly counter-productive details that would never have been included, unless the story really happened that way. All the Gospels, especially the first three, read like unedited history. Later, so-called gospels (e.g., The "Gospel" of Thomas), were significantly and obviously edited and theologized for the authors' philosophical and/or religious purposes.

But the New Testament Gospels appear to be relentlessly true to the story as it happened. For example, the writers didn't attempt to smooth out apparent disparities in their respective descriptions of the same events in Jesus' life. Many have noticed how the details surrounding Jesus' resurrection vary slightly between Gospel accounts. While these disparities can be reconciled with integrity, the lack of early attempts to synthesize these apparent differences reveals how the various writers simply recorded what they or eye witnesses saw, without trying to make all the pieces fit together.

Another example of the Gospels simply recording the facts as they happened is the way they elucidate the antics of Peter, Jesus' lead apostle. If I were trying to craft a story to showcase the leaders I wanted people to follow, I'd do my best to show them in the best possible light. But the Gospels record several of Peter's public blunders (e.g., not having enough faith to walk on water with Jesus, babbling so foolishly that God's voice booms from heaven telling him to shut up, and his triple denial of Jesus on the eve of His crucifixion). None of these events give us confidence in Peter as a leader; yet, the grittiness of these accounts suggest they must have actually happened, or else they would not have been included in the record.

In addition to Peter's failures, the recording of the apostles fleeing in fear when Jesus is arrested, alongside their regular outbursts of anger, foolishness and lack of faith, make it clear that the Gospel writers told the life and times of Jesus as they saw it, without any agenda-driven varnish.

And then there is Jesus' politically incorrect relationship with His female disciples. Most striking is the assertion that the resurrected Jesus appeared to the women disciples before the men. This claim by the Gospel writers was highly offensive to the cultural sensitivities of their audience. The only reason they would have included this part of the story is if it actually happened.

3. The Gospels are replete with historical data (e.g., people, places and events) that correspond perfectly with confirmed archaeological discoveries about first century Palestine. In many cases, the Gospels have been the sole and best source of archaeological data from that period, until later corroborated by other archaeology.

4. All the Gospels were completed within the lifetime of eyewitnesses who easily could have refuted the authors' claims, had they been false. This fact becomes even more significant when we consider that the contents that ended up in the Gospels were being recorded, collected and protected from the earliest days after Jesus's departure. This means the authors of the Gospels would have been accountable to eyewitnesses who heard the words and saw the deeds of Jesus. Such corroboration ensured the historicity of the Gospels.

5. The disciples of Jesus, especially the apostles and Gospel writers, followed Jesus at great peril. In first-century Palestine and throughout the Roman Empire, Christians were a persecuted minor-

ity. Remember, Jesus was rejected and murdered by the masses. History and tradition confirm that all the apostles were eventually murdered for their beliefs about Jesus (with the possible exception of John, who was exiled to the Isle of Patmos by the Roman emperor, Domitian). Many others were fed to wild beasts or lit on fire to illuminate Nero's garden, simply because they followed Jesus.

Why do these historical facts matter? Because they remove any "personal gain" motivation that might have persuaded the Gospel writers to fudge the data to gain political power. The fact is, they had no personal power or comfort to gain; instead, they had everything to lose by recording and defending the words and deeds of Jesus. Countless others died to defend the content they faithfully recorded.

6. The bodily resurrection of the crucified Jesus was the central teaching of the first-century church and the centerpiece of Christian belief. I will talk more about the historical evidence for the resurrection of Jesus in the next chapter. For now, suffice it to say, Jesus predicted His death, burial and resurrection, and then did exactly as He promised.

He also promised to guide the apostles as they recalled and recorded His words (John 16:12-13). If He could rise from the dead, surely He could continue to guide them in accurately recording His life and ministry. The strength of this defense obviously rests on the evidence for the resurrection of Jesus. You can judge the facts for yourself when the time comes.

If you would like to take a closer look at the veracity of the New Testament documents and message, consider reading, *Can We Trust the Gospels?*, by Mark D. Roberts, a New Testament scholar from Harvard Divinity School. His book was published by Crossway Books in 2007.

Chapter 10

God-Man

We had planned this trip for months. Now, after driving eleven hours, with the Midwestern flatlands behind us, my son David and I were close to our destination—the Civil War battleground of Gettysburg.

In the pitch blackness of that rural Pennsylvania night, large raindrops pelted and covered our windshield, as we strained to navigate the winding mountain road. But we pressed on until, finally, we were there, welcomed to this sacred place by ghostly statues of fallen generals, barely visible in the moonlight, beckoning us to hear their story.

Over the next two days, we toured the entire battlefield, walking by the creek bed where Confederate soldiers snuck into Gettysburg, envisioning the Union response, standing on Little Round Top and picturing the fierce battle it hosted that hot July in 1863. We walked around buildings, encountered dozens of historical points and read countless plaques, as we tried to get our minds around the magnitude of this place.

We ended our tour where the battle for Gettysburg ended, on Cemetery Ridge. It was there the Union army held back 12,000 charging confederates, leaving 7,500 of them lying on the battlefield, turning the war against the South for good.[54] In total, "Confederate casualties in dead, wounded and missing were 28,000...Union casualties were 23,000..."[55]

Unfortunately, this was just one of many bloody battles in the Civil War. By the war's end, as many as 700,000 soldiers had been killed, making it the deadliest war in American history.[56]

Both the North and the South fought in the name of freedom, liberty and patriotism. Each claimed to champion these ideals and hold the higher moral ground to do so. For those in the

---

54 "The Battle of Gettysburg." The History Place, Nov. 2011 <http://www.historyplace.com/civilwar/battle.htm>.

55 IBID

56 "The Price in Blood." Civil War Potpourri, Nov. 2011 < http://www.civilwarhome.com/casualties.htm>

South, the reasons for the war were complex, not simply about fighting for the right to hold slaves.

But for many in the North, slavery was the fundamental issue of the war. Though striving to preserve the union in general, many in the North believed they were fighting against a dark and ancient practice that had too often stained human history.[57]

Few evils in our world evoke the scorn, emotion and resolve as the degrading practice of slavery. Defenders of human dignity have long opposed the practice of one human being owning another, as well as oppressive institutions that abuse certain classes of people. No wonder Jesus not only opposed such abuses, but used the concept of slavery to describe our plight as a fallen race.

This comparison makes all the more sense when you consider that, in the first-century Roman Empire, which included the Palestine of Jesus' day, at least one-third of the population was slaves.[58] People owning people was a way of life.

---

57 See for example, "Top Five Causes of the Civil War." About.com: American History, Nov. 2011 <http://americanhistory.about.com/od/civilwarmenu/a/cause_civil_war.htm>.

58 See for example, "Slavery in the Roman Empire." World History Blog, Dec 2011 ,http://www.worldhistoryblog.com/2005/06/slavery-in-roman-empire.html>.

Some had voluntarily agreed to work off a debt as temporary servants, but many were born or forced into slavery. Purchased at an auction, they were considered mere property, owned and controlled by their buyer.

By law, a slave owner had absolute authority over every part of his slave's life. A slave's children were the property of his master to do with as he pleased. A master could punish or even kill his "property" at will.

Without the money to purchase his freedom, a slave would be in debt to his owner forever—unless the owner chose to absorb the cost of freeing him, or another person purchased him and set him free. In other words, a slave couldn't taste freedom without a *redeemer*, someone who had the resources and desire to do for him what he could not do for himself.

Imagine what it would feel like to be a slave, to be owned and controlled by another person, to long for freedom but taste only oppression. What if you were *born* into slavery, never knowing what it's like to be free, believing that bondage to another is just the way things are.

Now imagine being told that bondage you assumed was normal is, in reality, completely abnormal. Can you imagine learning that you were meant to live an entirely different kind of life, one free from oppression and filled with hope and creative expression, as well as dignified, eye-to-eye community with all people?

Having been born into slavery, you might scoff at such a possibility or wonder how you could ever be liberated. But deep down, you would hope. At the core of your being, you'd long to be free, to express your full humanity.

No wonder Jesus used the imagery of slavery to describe our plight as a fallen race. If the story Jesus told is true, we enslaved ourselves to sin through the fall, and found ourselves spiritually bankrupt and justly condemned. Crushed under the weight of our sin, we are unable to escape our self-imposed bondage to this darkness. We lack the resources to purchase our freedom, to right our wrong or conquer the evil that owns us.

And so we settle for the slavery that defines us. We succumb to the bondage that degrades our humanity and keeps us from enjoying shalom.

Thankfully, God sent a Redeemer to do for us what we could not do for ourselves—one with the desire and resources to pay our debt by removing our guilt, and to set us free to live again.

Jesus often used the language of slavery and freedom to describe His role as Messiah, saying of Himself, ...the Son of Man came not to be served but to serve, and to give his life as a ransom for many.

...you will know the truth, and the truth will set you free.

"I am the way, the truth and the life. No one comes to the Father except by me." [59]

Jesus claimed to be the only one who can set us free from the slavery we've come to think of as normal. I'm convinced that He is, in fact, the hero of the ancient story we find ourselves in, and the only One who can take us back to Eden.

A unique Champion

Jesus is uniquely qualified to redeem (lift us) from the fall, because of *who* He is and *what* He did to make us free.

Luke traces Jesus' genealogy all the way back

59 Matthew 20:28; John 8:32; John 14:6, respectively

to Adam.[60] But even though Jesus entered Adam's fallen race, He claimed a perfect moral authority for Himself, based on His assertion that He was more than just a man. Specifically, He claimed to be the one and only *God-man*—fully God and fully human. He was a single person existing in two natures: human and divine. In the words of the Apostle John, "God became flesh"[61] in the person of Jesus Christ.

My spirit soars with wonder as I ponder this, the greatest and most beautiful mystery in history. In very clear terms, Jesus claimed He possessed the very nature, glory and authority of God.[62] He asserted the right to forgive sins as God,[63] and even received worship as God.[64]

But Jesus Christ was also fully human. He had human thoughts, feelings and bodily life. His humanity was just like ours, except that, He was perfect and we are not. This is because His

60 Luke 3:23-38

61 John 1:14

62 See for example, John 10:30-31, 17:1-5;

63 Mark 2

64 Matthew 13:32-34; John 20:26-29; Revelation

divine nature perfected His human nature, without minimizing or changing His humanity or His deity.

As predicted by Old Testament prophecy, Jesus' mother, Mary, became pregnant with Him before having relations with any man. Matthew quotes God's promise, given through the Prophet Isaiah:

> Behold, the virgin shall conceive and bear a son, and they shall call his name Immanuel, which means "God with us."[65]

Luke affirms that Mary miraculously conceived Jesus by the Holy Spirit. This is why He was called the "Son of God,"[66] for Jesus, the man, embodied the very nature of God.

Think of it. God Himself entered our fallen race, to release us from spiritual slavery and teach us to sing again. The Creator became part of His creation. The infinite God wrapped Himself in finite humanity. This cannot be, we say to ourselves. It blows all of our mental categories and defies explanation. This mystery is as profound

65 Matthew 1:22

66 Luke 1:35

as it is beautiful, as shocking as it is wonderful, magnifying God's kindness and reminding us of our worth.

But isn't something like this exactly what we should expect if God made us for Himself and promised to lift us from our fall?

Our Champion is God Himself! He became one of us to do for us what we could not do for ourselves—bring us back into a face-to-face relationship with Him. As the perfect man, Jesus could stand before God the Father as our representative. As the infinite God, His infinite value gave Him infinite resources to fix what we've broken. Only the God-man was qualified to lift us from the fall and take us back to Eden. This becomes more clear as we look at what He had to do to set us free.

A unique mission

It was the most scandalous and controversial event in history. On a Friday afternoon in March of 30 A.D., the Roman government executed three men by crucifixion. Two were violent criminals. The other was accused of healing the sick, raising the dead, forgiving sins, and claiming to be God's Messiah.

Why was Jesus crucified alongside men like these? Thousands had loved Him. Most who knew Him hung onto His every word and marveled at His deeds. But the religious elite despised Jesus. His massive popularity had challenged their authority, weakened their prestige and exposed their self-serving motives.

The final straw came when Jesus challenged those in charge of the most powerful symbol in Jerusalem—the temple. Jesus publicly rebuked the temple leaders for commercializing worship into a money-making venture. He assumed authority over the temple and ultimately claimed He was superior to the temple, because temple worship pointed to Him, the long-awaited Messiah.[67]

Why Did Many Jew Reject Jesus as Messiah?

To be fair, the religious power brokers were looking for the Messiah, too. But they assumed He would support the establishment and extend their prestige as its leaders. When Jesus stood against them, they insisted He was standing against God and convinced the masses He deserved to die.

So there Jesus was. Having been brutally beaten, mocked and reviled, his enemies had nailed

67 Matthew 12:5, 21:12-13

His hands and feet to a wooden cross, where He died a slow, excruciating death by crucifixion.

But all this was part of God's perfect plan for our rescue. Jesus repeatedly told His disciples He had come to die and rise again in order to break the power of sin.[68] He came to seek and save the lost, to give His life as a ransom for many.

We must not think that the Jews or Romans are solely to blame for Jesus' death. In a very real sense, you and I hung Him there. *We* are the reason Jesus came, lived a perfect life, and voluntarily ended it on that ugly cross, at the hands of sinful men like you and me.

For, by God's design, in that tragic, breathtaking moment, the unthinkable happened. The sinless One, who is infinitely good, absorbed the full weight and consequence of our sin against Him. More specifically, "For our sake, [God] made Him to be sin who knew no sin ..."[69] that He (Jesus) might conquer our sin and purchase our forgiveness through his sacrificial death on our behalf.

As Jesus secured our forgiveness, the sky turned

68 See for example, Mark 8:30

69 2 Corinthians 5:21

dark.[70] Under the veil of this darkness, a private exchange took place between the Righteous Judge, God the Father, and Jesus Christ, God's Son. Crushed under the weight of the world's sin, the sinless Son of God affirmed by quoting prophetic scripture that He was fulfilling God's promise to save us.

In anguish, He cried out, "My God, my God, why have you forsaken me?!"[71] In this horribly beautiful moment of infinite mercy, justice and grace, God the Father laid the sin of the world on His sinless Son, and Jesus bore God's condemnation for our rebellion against Him. Fulfilling God's ancient promise, the Messiah dove headfirst into the vortex of evil to break its crushing hold upon us, to turn us right-side out, that we might shine in His presence once again.

But why did our rescue require the Messiah's death? The answer is simple, but it requires courage to face. God warned Adam and Eve that the result of sin is death.[72] He made this clear from

---

70 Luke 23:24-25

71 Matthew 27:46. Jesus was quoting from Psalm 22, a clearly Messianic Psalm that points to Him.

72 Genesis 2:17

the beginning. "Follow me and live. Rebel against me and you will smash yourself against a perfect justice that will require your spiritual and physical death."

Adam and Eve, and the entire human race with them, died *spiritually* (became separated from God) when they rebelled against Him in Eden. Because of their spiritual death, their bodies deteriorated and died *physically*, introducing mortality into the human experience. But this was not the way God wanted the story to end, so He sent His Son to crush the power of sin and reverse the effects of the fall, in order to put an end to spiritual and physical death.

And so, after living a sinless life, Jesus died as if he were a sinner. By God's design, Jesus' righteous death paid the penalty that we, not He, deserved, that we might receive the righteousness that He, not we, possessed. His sacrifice broke the back of sin's power to condemn, enslave and separate us from God.

The sacrificial death of the God-man is as mysterious as it is beautiful. His *physical* death was beyond excruciating. We struggle to imagine the pain

He felt as He died. But the *spiritual* death He endured on that cross is beyond our comprehension.

Without a doubt, evil cost God infinitely more than it would ever exact from the human race. Upon the cross, the Son of God was separated from God the Father for the first and only time in eternity. This part of the story is so unthinkable, so impossible, it brings me to my knees.

In the moment Jesus cried out, "My God, my God, why have you forsaken me?," He was bearing my sin and yours, and therefore experiencing the judgment and rejection of God the Father that we, not He, deserved.

Imagine how the infinite heart of God must have broken in that moment. Before the Son of God entered humanity, He had enjoyed an eternal embrace with His Father. The very nature of God is bound up in the relationship between the Father and the Son.[73] Their love and affection for one another are infinite and impenetrable, which means the relational separation they experienced in Jesus' dark moment on the cross was inconceivably and infinitely painful.

---

73 Together with the Holy Spirit, The Father and the Son make up the Triune Godhead. See the toggle from chapter five, entitled, "What is the Trinity?" for more detail.

The Bible teaches that hell is a place of everlasting separation from God.[74] In that moment of separation from His Father, the God-man experienced more hell than could ever be experienced by the entire human race, if we all spent forever there. The Son of God willfully tasted an infinite measure of spiritual death (hell) for us, so that we don't have to.

At the cross of Jesus Christ, we see the intersection of God's perfect justice and His boundless mercy. As a perfect judge, He could not allow our rebellion to go unpunished. To ensure we would not be judged forever, He mercifully judged His sinless Son in our place.

In those dark moments on the cross, Jesus voluntarily endured infinite suffering to pay the infinite penalty for our rebellion against God. In His death on our behalf, Jesus took all of sin's condemnation upon Himself, leaving no condemnation for us. He dismantled sin's power to condemn us, own us or control us, as He broke the back of evil forever.

The cross of Jesus reminds me that God knows all about suffering—undeserved and infinite suf-

74 2 Thessalonians 1:5-10

fering. Jesus Christ, God in the flesh, absorbed the evil of this world in order to conquer it. This truth melts any doubts about God's goodness and gives me hope and strength to face the toughest questions in life. I may not understand why the effects of the fall wreak this or that havoc on the earth. I may not get why God intervenes to protect some, but not others, from the horrors of suffering, disease and abuse in our fallen world. But when I look at the cross, I cannot doubt God's goodness or love.

Other stories (religions) ask us to ignore, accept or surrender to evil. But Jesus, our Champion, invaded evil at its highest point and endured its most powerful blow, in order to crush it once and for all and take us back to Eden.

Remember God's promise to Adam and Eve in Genesis 3:15? Speaking to the devil about a future battle with God's Messiah, God says, "He (Messiah) shall bruise your (devil's) head, and you (devil) shall merely bruise his heel." This is exactly what happened at the cross, where the real losers were the devil, and evil itself. This becomes even more clear when we understand that the death of our evil-crushing Champion wasn't the end of the story. It was just the beginning.

Setting us free from our bondage to the fall, Jesus not only endured a death He did not deserve, but as we'll see in the next chapter, He conquered death forever, so that, in His words, "If the Son sets you free, you will be free indeed."[75]

75 John 8:36

Why Did Many Jews Reject Jesus as Messiah?

To begin, remember that the first followers of Jesus were Jewish. Thousands of faithful Jews who understood the teaching about the coming Messiah in the Old Testament believed that Jesus was this Messiah. Even so, most of the Jewish elite rejected Jesus, not merely because they were stubborn or self-serving. They had theological and practical reasons for rejecting Jesus when He came.

In their defense, the Jewish leaders knew the Old Testament prophecies which taught that the Messiah would bring complete peace on earth. They expected the Messiah to judge between the nations and decide disputes. They also anticipated that, under the Messiah's leadership, all people would beat their swords into plowshares and their spears into pruning hooks, and that countries would not "learn war anymore" (Isaiah 2:4). In addition, the Prophet Isaiah declared, regarding the Messiah:

> Righteousness shall be the belt of his waist, and faithfulness the belt of his loins. The wolf shall

> dwell with the lamb, and the leopard shall lie down with the young goat, and the calf and the lion and the fattened calf together; and a little child shall lead them. The cow and the bear shall graze; their young shall lie down together; and the lion shall eat straw like the ox. The nursing child shall play over the hole of the cobra, and the weaned child shall put his hand on the adder's den. They shall not hurt or destroy in all my holy mountain; for the earth shall be full of the knowledge of the LORD as the waters cover the sea. (Isaiah 11:5-9 ESV)

Isaiah was clear in this and other prophecies, that the Messiah would usher in an era of unprecedented, universal and unchallenged peace on the earth.

In chapter nine, we looked at Jesus' quotation from Isaiah 61 that speaks of Messiah's reign on earth, and how Jesus claimed that this prophecy was fulfilled in Him. However, while quoting this passage (see Luke 4:16-19), Jesus stopped the quotation immediately before a line from the Isaiah passage that spoke of the Messiah bringing judgment on the world and establishing His political reign of peace on earth.

In other words, Jesus saw Himself as Messiah, but He came to Earth at that time to fulfill a portion, not all, of what He would ultimately do as Messiah. Throughout His ministry, Jesus called people to enter the Kingdom of God that had come through Him (see for example, Matthew 3:2; 4:23; 5:3, 10; Mark 10:15; Luke 6:20). And yet, even though He had brought the Kingdom with Him spiritually, Jesus taught His disciples that He would come a second time, at the end of the age, to finish His job as Messiah, by judging the living and the dead and creating a new heavens and earth where only righteousness dwells (Matthew 19:28; 24:29-31; 2 Peter 3:8-13; Revelation 19-21).

So Jesus saw His Messianic mission taking place in two phases. At His first coming, He brought spiritual renewal to His people, calling them to enter the Kingdom spiritually. At His second coming, He will bring the geo-political peace that many Jews of His day expected from the Messiah when He appeared the first time.

The Messianic prophecies of the Old Testament affirm this two-stage unfolding of the Messianic Kingdom. For example, in Isaiah 53, the prophet declares that the Messiah, who would one day bring perfect peace to the earth, must first suffer and die to bring spiritual healing and renewal to His people. Likewise, the prophet Daniel foresaw that Messiah would be "cut off" (killed) shortly after He appeared on the earth (Daniel 9:26). But, according to Daniel, the very same Messiah will return at the end of the age as a conquering King, to set up His Kingdom on the earth (Daniel 7:13-14).

Both Isaiah and Daniel envisioned two stages in the Messiah's work—the first ending in His apparent defeat, and the second ending with the realization that He is and will be victorious forever.

We see the same pattern in Psalm 22, which foretells the death and resurrection of the Messiah. Similarly, The Prophet Zechariah predicts that those who had "pierced" (killed) the Messiah will see Him return in glory, as their risen judge, at the end of the age (Zechariah 12:10).

Likewise, the prophets Jeremiah and Ezekiel speak of a purely spiritual role the Messiah would play in forgiving sins, cleansing His people and giving them new hearts. This work would be in conjunction with, but distinct from, the Messiah's geo-political reign on the earth at the end of the age.

It seems the Old Testament prophets foresaw a dual aspect of Messiah's Kingdom-bringing work. He would bring spiritual renewal to His people through His death and resurrection; AND, he will reign unchallenged as King on the earth at the end of the age. Jesus' words, deeds and predictions fit this storyline perfectly.

But it seems the Jewish leaders of Jesus' day were primarily interested in the political reign of Messiah on the earth, perhaps because they had been serving Rome for almost one-hundred years. Before that, they'd been enslaved to other nations for six-hundred years, except for an important, though brief, period of independence, won through what was known as the Maccabean revolution in 165 B.C., less than two-hundred years earlier.

With this political revolution in their rearview mirror, the religious leaders of Jesus' day longed for a new revolution that would set their nation free for good. But Jesus called them first to embrace spiritual renewal, and wait for final political renewal at the end of the age.

Chapter 11

The Death of Death

It was a milestone no one else saw. Debbie and I were celebrating our eighteenth anniversary. Most couples focus on silver or golden celebrations. But the number "18" carried more significance for me than any other anniversary could.

For you see, at eighteen years, my wife and I were putting to death a legacy of divorce (my parents were divorced after eighteen years of marriage) and bringing to life a legacy of enduring love. Ten years later, in our twenty-eighth year of marriage, we're growing a legacy of love and devotion to pass on to our children and generations to come.

But make no mistake, both legacies have profoundly shaped my life. The old legacy rocked my confidence in the institution of marriage and made me wonder if enduring love was possible. The new legacy has replaced the old with renewed confidence and hope for the future.

As I reflect on the idea of breaking and making legacies, I'm reminded of our Champion, Jesus. If the story He told is true, our fall from shalom in Eden enslaved us to a legacy of brokenness and sin. From life to death—how far we fell.

Thankfully, God promised that this legacy of darkness would not define us forever. Through His Christ, He would break and replace this legacy of death with a legacy of enduring life. Specifically, He would make all things new through two events that would pierce the darkness with brilliant, transforming light.

We've already talked about the first event—Jesus' sacrificial death, through which He broke the back of sin. The second came three days later, when Jesus rose bodily from the dead.

I'm convinced that, just as the prophets foretold and Jesus predicted,[76] our Champion died on a cross but lived to tell the story—and that changes everything. For, if Jesus rose from the dead, He has conquered death and proven He can bring us new

76 See for example, Psalm 22; Isaiah 53; Zechariah 12:10; Matthew 17:22-23; 20:17-19.

life. He has ushered in a new era, a new beginning, a way for us to taste the shalom of Eden once again.

Jesus said that, at the end of the age, God will dissolve and recreate the heavens and the earth into a realm where only righteousness dwells.[77] All who are His will be fully alive and with Him forever in this new Eden. Between now and then, He offers those who are His a down-payment on this new creation, granting us new *spiritual* life, as we await the renewal of all things at the end of the age. All this is possible because Jesus conquered and reversed the curse of sin through His death and resurrection from the dead. Let's take a closer look at this event that changed everything.

On multiple occasions, Jesus told His disciples that He had come for one purpose—to die and rise again, and thereby conquer the condemnation and control of sin in our fallen world.[78] In a bold promise, He declared:

> ...I lay down my life that I may take it up again. No one takes it from me, but I lay it down of

77 Matthew 19:28. See also 2 Peter 3:8-13 and Revelation 21.

78 Matthew 17:22-23; 20:17-19; Mark 9:31; Luke 18:31

> my own accord. I have authority to lay it down, and I have authority to take it up again.[79]

I love how Jesus set an impossible standard for Himself and then pulled it off. But isn't this exactly what we'd expect from our Hero, an impossible rescue in the real world?

The bodily resurrection of Jesus from the dead proved beyond any doubt that He is God's Messiah, and God's Kingdom (newness of life) has come to us through Him.

The Apostle Paul was the most well-known follower of Jesus in the years immediately following Jesus' life and ministry. He wrote much of the New Testament of the Bible. Paul understood that without Jesus' bodily resurrection from the dead, Christianity would be a religious sham, and all followers of Jesus would be fools. He wrote:

> ...if Christ has not been raised, then our preaching is in vain and your faith is in vain... if Christ has not been raised, your faith is futile and you are still in your sins. If in Christ we have hope

79 John 10:17b-18; See also John 2:19-21

> in this life only, **we are of all people most to be pitied.**[80]

Our hope is not simply in the *teachings* of Jesus, but in His redemptive work on the cross and resurrection from the dead.

Jesus didn't come to establish a new morality or code of ethics. He came to conquer the condemning ownership and control of sin over the fallen race of Adam. He came to pay the death penalty for our sin and rise from the dead to break sin's power. If all He did was live, teach and die like any other man, then we are still "in our sins" and without hope. But if Jesus rose from the dead, then He was who He claimed to be: God's Messiah, our Champion who makes all things new.

With the Apostle Paul, I'm convinced the bodily resurrection of Jesus is a fact of history, the essence of our hope, and the climactic center of the story we find ourselves in. Some are skeptical of mankind's ability to reconstruct history with enough accuracy to live in light of it. But we make decisions based

80 1 Corinthians 15:14-19

on history all the time.[81] The question is how well our conclusions about history match the evidence before us, and whether we have the courage to follow the evidence where it leads, without allowing our biases to keep us from going there.

The evidence for Jesus' resurrection from the dead is clear and impressive. The fact that Jesus' tomb was empty on the Sunday following His Friday execution is indisputable. His appearances to eyewitnesses are well-documented. And the transformation of the disciples can only be explained if Jesus actually rose from the dead. For these reasons, I believe that, just as Jesus predicted and His followers have celebrated for nearly two-thousand years, Jesus rose bodily from the dead. And that changes everything.

Johnny, Dave and I talked about how other sto-

---

81 For example, though we may not have been alive to witness it, we believe that Martin Luther King, Jr. launched a civil rights movement in the 1960's that still shapes our country today. In the same way, though none of us were there, we believe that John Hancock signed the Declaration of Independence in July of 1776. We draw all sorts of conclusions about people like Napoleon, Julius Caesar, Darwin, and Henry the VIII, based on historical evidence. Claims about history are neither impossible nor meaningless. The question is how well our conclusions fit the evidence before us.

ries (religions) base their claims on *un*verifiable spiritual experiences or ideas of others.[82] But the Jesus story stands or falls on this very public, verifiable event in history. Maybe you have pre-concluded that events such as a resurrection from the dead can't happen. But if you have the courage to follow the smoke to the flame, you may find the evidence leading you in this impossible direction.

Few doubt that Jesus was murdered by professional executioners that Friday afternoon. Or that His dead body was placed in a rock tomb early that evening.

More importantly, there is no doubt that Jesus' tomb was *empty* the following Sunday morning. We have no record of eye-witnesses denying that the body of Jesus was missing. Instead, the empty tomb seems to have been universally and openly acknowledged without controversy. The important question is: "How did the tomb that held Jesus' dead body on Friday evening became empty by Sunday morning?"

The disciples claimed Jesus rose from the dead and interacted with them for many days. They suffered greatly to defend this claim. Many lost

82 E.g., Hinduism, Buddhism, Islam

their lives. But they were certain they had talked to, eaten with and spent real time alongside their resurrected Messiah, and they were compelled to proclaim that reality.

The bodily resurrection of Jesus wasn't just a mystical idea or sentimental afterthought by those who followed Him. It was the basis for the disciples' trust in Him. When they proclaimed that Jesus had raised bodily from the dead, they were making a fact claim. They did so when other eyewitnesses could have refuted their assertion with contrary evidence. But nobody did.

This fact is especially significant when you consider that both the Jews and Romans were highly motivated to crush the Jesus revolution—the Jews, because they rejected Him as Messiah, and the Romans, because the rapidly growing "Jesus sect" was challenging the religions of Rome that were deeply embedded in every aspect of Roman life.

Given that the Jesus movement was based on the core belief that Jesus had risen bodily from the dead, the religious and political leaders would have tried valiantly to refute this claim. Interestingly, neither offered a credible alternative explanation for Jesus' empty tomb, though the Jewish leaders made a feeble attempt to falsely accuse Jesus' disciples of stealing his body.

> ...some of the guard went into the city and told the chief priests all that had taken place. And when they had assembled with the elders and taken counsel, they gave a sufficient sum of money to the soldiers and said, "**Tell people, 'His disciples came by night and stole him away while we were asleep**.' And if this comes to the governor's ears, we will satisfy him and keep you out of trouble." So they took the money and did as they were directed. And this story has been spread among the Jews to this day.[83]

The Resurrection of Jesus in History

This story was never taken seriously, because it was so implausible.

Where did these brave, body-stealing disciples of Jesus come from? After He was arrested, virtually all of them ran and hid. Peter followed Jesus from a distance, only to deny Him publicly three times."[84] This is hardly the mettle required from those who would brazenly steal Jesus' body, by overpowering

83 Matthew 28:11-15

84 Mark 14:43-50; Luke 22:47-62

well-trained soldiers[85] guarding His tomb, which was carved into the side of a mountain.

And why would Jesus' disciples *want* to steal His body to make it look like He'd risen from the dead if, in fact, He hadn't? Wouldn't propagating this deception dishonor their teacher by going against everything He stood for?

More importantly, their faith and message rested on a fully alive, resurrected Jesus. Why would they stage this farce and then voluntarily die for a lie that gained them nothing?

Finally, given the immense persecution they experienced for their claim, surely one of them would have broken under the pressure and spilled the beans. But they stood by their claim, undaunted, declaring that Jesus had risen from the dead.

In the toggle, *The Resurrection of Jesus is History,* I point to the Apostle Paul's quotation of an ancient creed that declared the death, burial and resurrection of Jesus. The dating of this creed shows that Jesus' followers were proclaiming his resurrection in or near 30 A.D., the year He was pub-

85 Matthew 27:62-66

licly executed and buried.[86]

Additional information Paul received with the creed asserts that, after appearing to the apostles several times in various ways, the resurrected Jesus appeared to more than five-hundred people at once. Paul wrote that many of these witnesses were still alive 25 years later. "Go ask the eyewitnesses," Paul implies. "They saw Jesus alive from the dead."

From the beginning, Jesus' resurrection was treated by those who claimed to follow Him as a verifiable, historical event. People were encouraged to investigate the resurrection story for themselves. Many did, and were never the same.

One of the most beautiful affirmations of Jesus' resurrection is the dramatic transformation of His disciples after they saw Him alive, following his crucifixion. Apart from Jesus' resurrection, it's impossible to explain their dramatic change. When the Romans arrested, tried and executed

86 This date is the consensus conclusion of most New Testament scholars. For a solid treatment of this and other aspects of the historicity of Jesus' resurrection (including bibliographical support), see William Lane Craig's, The Son Rises, Wipf and Stock Publishers, 1981.

their Master, they went into hiding, terrified and disillusioned.

But then, almost overnight, they became courageous and focused men and women, filled with unquenchable hope and zeal. They gave up all they had to proclaim that Jesus had risen from the dead. They suffered great loss and endured immense persecution. Eleven of the twelve apostles died martyrs deaths, because they believed and proclaimed the Jesus story.

This once sorry band of outcasts launched a movement so powerful it rocked the ancient world, and we're still feeling the tremors today. What drove the disciples' radical transformation? They claimed they had seen Jesus alive from the dead—and that changed everything.

Isn't this the miracle we've been longing for? Hoping for? Doesn't the resurrection of Jesus satisfy the deepest expectations in our hearts?

Discovering that Jesus conquered sin and death takes us back to the hope we once knew but somehow lost, to the ancient melody we sang together long ago. How liberating to sing again, to celebrate our Champion who broke sin's grip on us, that we might rise with Him and journey back to Eden. He died and rose to life that we might experience re-genesis—regeneration, brand new life as we were meant to live it, alive together with Him. No wonder Jesus boldly claimed to be our only hope when he said,

> "I am the way, and the truth, and the life. No one comes to the Father except through me."[87]

Some are offended by the idea that we need such radical renewal, and that only the death, burial and resurrection of Jesus can bring it. But the truth often hurts before it heals. It takes courage to embrace a truth we would rather suppress—that we are a fallen, broken people; that all is not well on Planet Earth; that we cannot save ourselves or turn things around on our own.

We need an extreme makeover of the soul, a new heart, complete renewal from the One with the resources and will to remake us. We need the life we lost when we disconnected ourselves from Him. We experience this life again when God reconnects us to Himself, by uniting us to our resur-

87 John 14:6

rected Champion through faith.

Without spiritual rebirth, we cannot return to life in Eden. But when God opens our eyes, captures our hearts, and awakens our faith in Him, we are changed forever. The lights come on when we reconnect to the One whose image we bear. It's as if we see life in color for the first time, as our broken hearts begin to mend.

Without the resurrection of Jesus, none of this would be possible. We would still be buried under the weight of our sin, and the ancient story would not have delivered on its promise. But if Jesus is raised from the dead, that changes everything. We have found our Champion. With Him, we can rise from death to life. We can return to Eden and sing again.

The Resurrection of Jesus is History

In 55A.D., the Apostle Paul wrote a letter to Christians in the ancient city of Corinth. In this letter, he quoted a creed he had received two decades earlier from the earliest followers of Jesus. These first Christians had formulated this statement of faith so they could recite together their belief in the death, burial and resurrection of Jesus Christ. Paul integrated their creed into his letter to the Christians at Corinth.

> For I delivered to you as of first importance what I also received: **that** Christ died for our sins in accordance with the Scriptures, **that** he was buried, **that** he was raised on the third day in accordance with the Scriptures, and **that** he appeared to Cephas, then to the twelve. Then he appeared to more than five hundred brothers at one time, most of whom are still alive, though some have fallen asleep. Then he appeared to James, then to all the apostles. (1 Corinthians 15:3-7 ESV)

The four statements beginning with "**that**" make up the heart of the ancient creed Paul quotes. The last paragraph includes additional information he received from the Jerusalem apostles when he received the creed from them sometime between 33-36 A.D.[1]

This creed is widely accepted as authentic and thought to have originated in Jerusalem between 30-35 A.D.* This is important for many reasons. Most importantly, it shows that belief in the resurrection of Jesus wasn't an afterthought, but the core belief of the very first Christians.

We know that the creed originated within just a few years of Christ's crucifixion, because Paul received it no later than 36 A.D., when he traveled to Jerusalem to meet Peter and James (Paul outlined his travel itinerary in a letter to the church in Galatia. See Galatians 1:11-2:10).

It's possible that Paul received this creed even earlier, while he was in Damascus between 33-36 A.D. Bottom line: This ancient creed could have been written before 33 A.D., but not after 36 A.D. This matters because Jesus was crucified in 30 A.D., which means that this formal creed declaring His death, burial and resurrection was

1 These dates are widely accepted by scholars. See William Lane Craig, *The Son Rises*, Wipf and Stock Publishers, 1981, p. pp. 46-48.

already circulating within three-to-six years after His death. And because a creed is a formulation of existing beliefs, the disciples must have believed these things about Jesus well before they formulated them into a creedal statement.

For example, if it took two-to-three years for the disciples to see the need for a creed and agree on the wording to express their existing beliefs, and we know the creed was written between 33-36 A.D., then belief in these things about Jesus began within zero-to-four years after his death in 30 A.D. This adds tremendous veracity to the Gospel accounts declaring the disciples believed Jesus rose from the dead three days after He was crucified in 30 A.D. We may deduce at least three things from this historical data:

1. As already stated, the death, burial, and resurrection of Jesus comprised the heart of the Jesus story from 30 A.D. forward. It was not an afterthought or tradition that was added later.

2. Belief in the death, burial and resurrection of Jesus happened way too early to be part of a myth or legend. Moreover, the existence of so many eyewitnesses "...would act as a safeguard against unhistori-

cal legends... [and] Legends do not arise significantly until the generation of eyewitnesses dies off. Hence, legends are given no ground for growth as long as witnesses are alive who remember the facts."[2] The earliest believers in Jesus' resurrection were compelled by real-time evidence, under the scrutiny and persecution of countless eyewitnesses, many of whom were motivated to refute their claim.

3. The multiple appearances of Jesus strengthen the historicity of His resurrection. In addition to His appearance to the women at the tomb (Luke 24:1-12), the creed records that Jesus appeared to Cephas (the former name of the Apostle Peter), and to the twelve apostles (more than once, according to the Gospels). The tradition Paul received with the creed says Jesus then appeared to more than five-hundred eyewitnesses at one time, and again to the apostles.

With so many people seeing the resurrected Christ in so many contexts over time, the possibility that people were hallucinating or fabricating the story of Jesus' resurrection approaches zero. They all affirmed that they had seen Jesus alive

---

2 William Lane Craig, *The Son Rises*, Wipf and Stock Publishers, 1981, p. 107.

after he'd been killed and buried. Paul says that many of the five-hundred-plus who saw the resurrected Jesus were still alive twenty-five years later when he wrote to the Corinthians.

By invoking this eye-witness testimony and essentially inviting his readers to confirm the resurrection of Jesus through those who saw Jesus alive after His execution, Paul affirms the historical ground of Jesus' resurrection.

One more thing makes the claims about Jesus' bodily resurrection historically significant. The Jewish understanding of resurrection was completely unlike what the disciples claimed happened to Jesus. N.T. Wright argues persuasively that only the bodily resurrection of Jesus, as recorded in the Gospels, can account for the view of Jesus' resurrection that gave birth to early Christian belief.[3] This is because the Jewish notion of resurrection in Jesus' day was much different than what the disciples of Jesus said happened to their leader.

The Jews were familiar with the idea of a per-

---

3 N.T. Wright, *Jesus' Resurrection and Christian Origins*, (Originally published in, Gregorianum, 2002, 83/4, 615–635. Found at: http://www.ntwrightpage.com/Wright_Jesus_Resurrection.htm.

son being "taken up" alive into heaven, as happened to Enoch and Elijah in the Old Testament. They were also familiar with the idea of departed spirits existing in a kind of shadowy, inaccessible underworld, awaiting the final resurrection. They also anticipated a universal resurrection from the dead of all deceased human beings at the end of the age, in which God would judge the living and the dead and establish His kingdom on earth.

But the idea of one dead man becoming alive again and living on the earth in a resurrection body had no precedent in Jewish theology or culture. Such an event would have been completely unexpected by those who claimed it had happened—and by those who heard their claims. And yet, it happened. A dead man became alive again and lived on the earth in a resurrection body. It was this story that gave birth to historical Christianity.

N.T. Wright concludes that the earliest (Gospel) accounts of Jesus' resurrection, "...challenge today's historian, as they challenged their first hearers, either to accept them or to come up with a better explanation for why Christianity began and why it took the shape it did."[4]

Finally, since the way in which Jesus rose from the dead was completely unexpected in first-century Palestine, we may conclude that those who claimed to see Jesus alive were not hallucinating, since this type of resurrection would not have been been part of their mental set of ideas to hallucinate from.[5]

The nature of Jesus' resurrection also argues against the idea that the disciples made the resurrection story up, or thought that, by making it up, they would be claiming something theologically significant that might persuade others to follow them.

The best conclusion from the evidence is that people weren't fabricating or hallucinating about anything. They simply reported what they saw, albeit strange and unexpected. Unless we begin with a settled bias against miracles, the evidence points firmly in the direction of a bodily resurrected Jesus. And that changes everything!

---

4 IBID

5 Craig argues extensively and persuasively that hallucination is not a reasonable explanation for the post-resurrection sightings of Jesus in *The Son Rises*, pp. 119-24.

Chapter 12

Fire Song

It was an f-bomb celebrated in heaven. Johnny, a South- Chicago boy, used the most powerful adjective in his native tongue to celebrate his new understanding of Jesus. "Jesus is ****ing IT!" he declared, wide eyed and animated. "Everything points to Him. He's the center of life!"

A few days later, sitting in my backyard, Johnny told me He wanted to follow Jesus.

"Are you sure?" I asked. "Jesus warns that following Him will make you a non-conformist revolutionary in a world that has fallen away from Him.[88] You may be rejected by people you care about if you set your heart to follow Jesus."

Johnny didn't miss a beat. "I know," he replied. "I'm ready to follow Him." Johnny had tasted the life Jesus offered and he was ready to drink deep-

88 John 15:18; Luke 14:25-27

ly—and that changed everything.

For starters, he's embarrassed about his F-bomb declaration about Jesus. I had to get his permission to tell you about it. He tells me he doesn't remember his colorful choice of words, perhaps because his language, like his life, has been so completely transformed.

Johnny had always been a gifted and winsome person, but when he came to the end of himself and found real life in Jesus Christ, he discovered what every follower of Jesus knows: We are never more alive, more human, or more of who we were created to be, than when we submit to the writer of our story. As someone has said, you become the very best version of yourself when you find yourself in Him.

Our friend Dave now follows Jesus, too. I've had a blast watching the lives of these two men fill with new vision, purpose and zeal. A good example of this transformation is the movie they were making when we first met at the Xtreme Bean coffee shop.

During their yearlong journey toward Jesus, they were working on an R-rated slasher film, complete with raunchy sex and gratuitous gore.

They'd invested nearly $300,000 and two years in the film. When the movie was finished and they began to evaluate distribution options, something remarkable happened.

One day, Johnny told me that he could no longer distribute the movie, because "it's not who we are anymore."

At tremendous financial loss, Dave agreed with Johnny, and they shelved the film.

But God made Johnny and Dave to be filmmakers. That's what they love and long to do—what they must do. Now, they're producing films to transform culture. In addition to pursuing feature film opportunities, they're looking for ways to partner with front-line justice organizations to raise awareness and money to stand against social evils like the child sex trade around the world.

Beautiful! I see Jesus in these men. Same guys; new hearts. Same artists; new vision. Same drive; new purpose.

Something similar happened to me during my senior year of high school. After a long spiritual hiatus, God awakened my heart through a friend who knew Jesus and introduced Him to me.

Chuck told me things I'd heard before but never fully understood. He spoke of Jesus, the Son of God, who died on a cross for my sins. He talked of my need for the forgiveness and renewal that only Jesus could bring.

Late one night, after several conversations covering a span of several weeks, we were cruising in his Toyota Corolla through the Metropolis of Eagle, Idaho (population 3,000 at the time), when Chuck asked me a question. "Given all you know about Jesus, what's keeping you from placing your trust in Him tonight?"

Funny he should ask, because in that moment, I could feel God wooing and capturing my heart. "Nothing," I answered.

Chuck pulled over and stopped the car. And right there on the side of the road, God gave me a new heart as I placed my faith in Him.

That moment changed everything for me. Like Johnny and Dave, I found my place in the story that defines and connects us with one another and, most importantly, with the God who made us for Himself. Don't get me wrong. I'm still a goofball who screws up and struggles with life. I still have questions, doubts and fears. There are many things I don't understand and I still have plenty of growing to do.

But since Jesus introduced Himself to me, things are only blurry on the edges of the page. In the center, all is clear. I know I was created by God, in His image, to enjoy Him forever. Like, you, I live in a fallen world. On my own, I am a sinner by nature and by choice. By myself, I could only push back on the One who made me to find my deepest joy in Him.

In His kindness, mercy and love, God sent a Messiah to lift me from my fall and conquer the power of my sin. By uniting me to Jesus Christ through faith, God has made me new. Because of Jesus, I am tasting shalom and looking forward to the final chapter of the story when *only* shalom will fill the earth.

Because I belong to God's Kingdom that has already come, but hasn't yet arrived in its fullness, I live in a beautiful tension. On the one hand, Jesus has made me new and God's Kingdom is expanding around me. On the other hand, I'm still broken and longing for the fullness of God's Kingdom to arrive. So I live today as one who knows the healing power of Jesus, as He reveals and mends my brokenness each day. At the same time, I long for Him to return and finish the job, when He ushers in perfect righteousness, goodness and shalom in the age to come.

My present-future hope compels me to point others to this joyful expectation in my broken world. By His power, I join the fight against evil, knowing it has been defeated and will one day be obliterated. Together with others who are His, I partner with Jesus the Revolutionary to bring purpose, hope and vision to those around me.

We listen to the lonely, feed the hungry, look for opportunities to defend the defenseless and speak for the voiceless. We remind ourselves and others that the Jesus story isn't just an ancient tale that encourages us to live better. It's the story of the One who makes me, you and everything new.

Finding my life in Jesus, I no longer need to define myself by what I do, who I know, my accomplishments, defeats, degrees, or associations. Apart from any of these things, I am His, so I am whole.

My communion with God restores my community with others, as I remember that *He* is God and

I am not, that life is about Him, not me, and that, the more I die to myself, the more I live in Him by loving and serving others. This is the beautiful paradox of the gospel. Jesus says,

> "Whoever seeks to preserve his life will lose it, but whoever loses his life will keep it."[89]

Again He says,

> "Whoever loves his life loses it, and whoever hates his life in this world will keep it for eternal life."[90]

These words seem upside-down in our fallen, self-centered world. But they reveal the right-side-up secret I've discovered to enjoying fullness of life in Him. Just like we experience more love when we give it away, we experience more life when we give *ourselves* away, first to Jesus, then to others.

We help others drink from the pool of life when we give ourselves away for them. Nowhere is this more obvious than when we forgive those who sin

89 Luke 17:33

90 John 12:25

against us. Jesus modeled this perfectly by giving Himself away for us when we deserved His judgment, not His mercy. Following His example, as I die to myself to live in Him, I'm free to forgive others who've sinned against me, remembering that no matter how much I'm called to forgive, God in Christ has forgiven me for immeasurably more.

Finally, the more I find myself in Him, the more I relish life as part of His story, in the majesty of His creation. Because I am His, every moment of my life is a sacred act of worshipful connection with my creator—enjoying my wife's beauty, tasting hops and barley brewed to perfection, hitting a golf ball, resonating with faithful middle C, feeling my chest thump from an over-amped bass guitar, or savoring the warmth of the sun, grit of the sand and coolness of the waves at the beach; Giving and receiving love with my wife and kids, singing off-key, telling bad jokes, helping a friend heal, or reminding a homeless woman of her worth—these are precious moments in life, through which I worship, reflect and enjoy the One who made me for Himself. I know that I was created to enjoy Him in a world that reflects His beauty, as part of *His* story that brings me my identity.

Now wide awake in Christ, I'm living under the down-payment of God's Kingdom today, as I await the fullness of His Kingdom to come. I join with all who are His in partnering with Jesus to bring hope to a world that's lost and dying without Him. We do this together as His people.

I'm inspired by Jesus-followers like my friend Chris, who loves to make money and give it away to make Jesus known. He's a Jesus-centered capitalist. His goal is to live off ten percent of his income, so he can give ninety percent to those in need. I see Jesus the Giver in him.

Peggy travels the world and works tirelessly in her own city to rescue and heal girls who've been kidnapped and mercilessly raped by pimps and johns. She also fights unjust legislation that penalizes these girls more than their abusers. I see Jesus the Just shining through her.

Brad and Josh spend their Wednesday nights teaching inner-city "pre-gang" kids about beauty, hope and life by showing them how to paint to music. These kids have very little beauty in their